Irish Proverbs

~

Traditional Wit & Wisdom

<small>SELECTED BY</small>
<small>FIONNUALA CARSON WILLIAMS</small>

<small>ILLUSTRATED BY MARLENE EKMAN</small>

Sterling Publishing Co., Inc
New York

In fond memory of my parents
Rosemary Moon Young of Ballymoney, County Antrim, and
Thomas Carson of Corraskea, County Monaghan
Maireann an chraobh...

An earlier, less detailed edition was published in 1992 by Poolbeg in Swords, County Dublin.

Library of Congress Cataloging-in-Publication Data

Williams, Fionnuala.
  Irish proverbs : traditional wit and wisdom / Fionnuala Williams.
    p.   cm.
  Includes index.
  ISBN 0-8069-3537-5
    1. Proverbs, Irish. I. Title.
  PN 6505.C5 I76   2000
  398.9'21'09417—dc21

                                          99-052780

10 9 8 7 6 5 4 3 2 1

Published by Sterling Publishing Company, Inc.
387 Park Avenue South, New York, N.Y. 10016
© 2000 by Fionnuala Carson Williams
Distributed in Canada by Sterling Publishing
C/o Canadian Manda Group, One Atlantic Avenue, Suite 105
Toronto, Ontario, Canada M6K 3E7
Distributed in Great Britain and Europe by Cassell PLC
Wellington House, 125 Strand, London WC2R 0BB, England
Distributed in Australia by Capricorn Link (Australia) Pty Ltd.
P.O. Box 6651, Baulkham Hills, Business Centre, NSW 2153, Australia
Manufactured in the United States of America
All rights reserved

Sterling ISBN 0-8069-3537-5

Contents

Preface

Although the following pieces of traditional advice—in the form of proverbs—were collected over 60 years ago, many are still used today. This is because proverbs survive over time if their message continues to be appropriate in the new era.

Most of the proverbs found in Ireland can also be found in various languages throughout many other countries of Europe. They can also be found in other continents where Europeans settled and so demonstrate cultural connections. As in other places, proverbs in Ireland can have a complex history and each would need to be studied individually to be certain of its journey between countries and languages.

The selection in this volume, unlike the majority of previous selections of proverbs from Ireland, was made from proverbs collected from oral tradition in the English language which, since the middle of the 19th century, has been the dominant language in most parts of Ireland. Many of them—for example, "Yellow butter tastes best"—have no obvious contemporary equivalents in England, while others—such as "Hunger is good kitchen"—differ from the standard English version. Sometimes the variation is because of local turns of phrase or words (such as "pratie" for "potato," "to hoke" for "to root," and "boreen" for "minor road") or because of the things mentioned in them: personal names (such as Carr, Ennis, O'Foy, Murphy, and Lord Leitrim) and place-names (like Ardee, Banagher, and Cork, not to mention the River Shannon), or typical plants (rushes and rowan) and food (champ, porridge, and stew).

Within Ireland the proverbs in both English and Irish enjoy a close relationship with one another, and the majority of those found in one language can also be found in the other. In the selection that follows are many that were first used exclusively in Irish and only came to have English versions in recent times. There are also those that were first used in Ireland in English and were then adopted into Irish. Then there are somewhat fewer that seem not to have passed into Irish at all.

In this book, Irish-language versions, where available, are given under the English. Many of the proverbs are exactly mirrored in the two languages; some vary and some appear to have no obvious published version in Irish. It is interesting that, in some cases, such as:

An old fox is shy of a trap,
Cha gheabhthar sean éan le cáith, [U]
Translation: An old bird is not caught with chaff,

English-language proverbs in Ireland have developed insular variants while the Irish-language version retains a more international form.

Ireland's long literary past as well as the influence of different languages have played their part in molding its proverbs, for example in the style known as the triad, in which three things are grouped—

Three things that are labor in vain:
throwing water on a drowned mouse,
whistling jigs to a milestone in the expectation of a dance
and ringing pigs in frosty weather.

This type of proverb was developed extensively in Irish literature, and it is certainly partly because of this that the style has continued in use in the proverbs in oral tradition until the twentieth century.

Turning to another style, the Wellerism, or quotation proverb—such as: "'Sour grapes,' says the fox when he couldn't catch the chicken"—is also represented in the English-language of Ireland. Some examples will be found in this selection, often at the start of each new section. Compared with the neighboring Scots, however, there are markedly fewer quotation proverbs in the English of Ireland. While it is well-known that quotation proverbs often allude to international folktales, the fact that some ordinary proverbs also do has been less discussed. Again, there are representatives of this in this selection—for instance, "The cat's one shift is worth all the fox's." Its meaning becomes clearer when it is realized that it refers to the international tale "The Cat's Only Trick." In this well-known tale in Ireland, the clever fox is, as usual, boasting— this time of his many ingenious tricks to a domestic cat. In the distance, a hunt is heard, and the cat quickly takes refuge up a tree. The fox, however, despite his many other abilities, cannot climb and is captured by the hunt. The presence of such proverbs suggests that the stories accompanying them were familiar to the proverb users and so gives an insight into the wider oral tradition.

The repertoire of proverbs used by any particular community reflects its concerns and values, and a great number of them draw their metaphors from everyday life. For this book I have purposely chosen proverbs that will give a flavor of rural life before the widespread mechanization and specialization of farming; where the images are taken from hearth and farm and not much further afield. As any proverb can be applied in a variety of situations, the proverbs here have been loosely arranged according to the scenes that they depict—such as butter making, sheep rearing, markets, and so on—rather than by what they mean or how they were applied. The sections have headings such as "Highroads and Byroads" and "Sport and Pastimes." Some sections, like "Food and Drinks" and "Farm Animals," are more extensive than others, for example "At the Mill" and "The Law." The length of each section to a certain extent reflects the relative amount of proverbs about certain subjects. While the images in the proverbs draw largely on the local surroundings familiar to the proverb users—the bogs and the green fields and hills with their whins and briars—they also contain fascinating references to the wider world, such as far-off places like America and Hanover, and to exotica, such as silks, satins, and velvet.

Many of the proverbs that follow, despite having been collected over half a century ago, will nevertheless be familiar to readers, because proverbs can be used to cover new situations. Nowadays as well as in everyday conversation, proverbs turn up in advertisments and are frequently used as newspaper headlines. "If you don't like the heat keep out of Miami," a variant of "If you don't want flour don't go into the mill," was spotted a few months ago promoting a gangster video, while "Good things often come in very small packages," which is also in this selection, was recently used in a Belfast newspaper to describe the magical performance of a company from The Small Theatre of Vilnius. The ability to weather the changing times is also shown in the last proverb of this book: "What the Pooka (a supernatural creature) writes let him read it himself." It was used this year about a ruling in the Northern Ireland Assembly in which those members who made contributions to the discussions in Irish or Ulster Scots, which are little spoken, as opposed to English, which would be understood by all, should provide their own translations. Proverbs live on!

Acknowledgments and Notes

The English-language proverbs in this book are published with the kind permission of Professor Séamas Ó Catháin of the Department of Irish Folklore, University College Dublin. They form part of the Schools' Collection Manuscripts, which date to the late 1930s. The proverbs were collected from oral tradition. This is the first time that a substantial number of them have appeared in print. They are given as in the original manuscripts with a few minor adjustments to punctuation and spelling.

The Irish-language equivalent proverbs are reprinted with the kind permision of An Gúm, Brainse na bhFoilseachán den Roinn Oideachais (publication branch of the Department of Education, Republic of Ireland). They are from the three main published collections of proverbs from oral tradition, each of which covers one of the following provinces: Connacht, Munster, and Ulster (see below for details). These cover a wider time span than those in English from the Schools' Collection: the majority belong to the first five decades of this century, but a few date back to the fifth decade of the last. Versions outside these three printed sources were not sought. They are indicated as follows: [C] for the Connacht collection, [M] for the Munster collection, and [U] for the Ulster collection. New editions of the Munster and Ulster collections, in which the Irish has been standarized, are in print and appear here. For the sake of consistency, the spelling in the Connacht collection has also been abbreviated in accordance with standard Irish, but neither the grammar nor lexis has been altered.

The Schools' Collection proverbs are shown in bold. Irish-language equivalents, where available, are next. If they vary, translations are placed in italics after each as shown below:

It is never hard to light a half-burned turf.
(English-language version from the Schools' Collection)
Is furas aibhleog a fhadú. [U]
(Irish-language version of the same proverb from printed source—the Ulster collection, in this case)
It is easy to light an ember.
(literal translation)

Even Irish-language versions, which vary much less than the previous example, have been translated, for example:

When the cat is out the mouse can dance.
Nuair bhíos an cat amuigh, bíonn cead rince ag na luchóga. [C]
When the cat is out the mice can dance. (literal translation)

Proverbs in Irish that show some variation from their English-language counterparts have been translated by Ciarán Ó Duibhín, whom I wish to thank not only for this but also for his valuable technical assistance, and by myself.

If a version exactly the same as the English-language proverb occurs in Irish, this is used; if not, then the next closest. Sometimes a synonym, such as:

Is fearr aon fhata amháin na lán pláta dhe chraicne.
One single potato is better than a plateful of skins. (literal translation)

for "**Better is a small fish than an empty dish**" is used when an exact equivalent is not available. Occasionally, a different proverb that expresses a similar sentiment has been included when the same one is not evident in Irish, for example:

Now I have a cow and a horse and everyone bids me good morrow

is followed by the nearest equivalent in Irish:

An té a bhíonn suas óltar deoch air is an té a bhíonn síos luítear cos air. [M]
He who is up his health is drunk and he who is down is trodden upon. (literal translation)

Sometimes several variants are listed together, for example:

There are long horns on the cows in Connacht.
Tá adharca fada ar bhuaibh i gConnachta. [U]

Kerry cows have long horns.

Cows in Meath have long horns.

Cows across the sea have long horns.
Bíonn adharca fada ar na ba thar lear. [C]

Far away cows have long horns but they often come home mileys.

Dialect words, such as "miley," which means "hornless cow," and farming practices are explained and occasionally specific usages are given for proverbs.

Key words found in the proverbs, both English and Irish, are indexed.

The three main published collections are:

An Seabhac, editor. *Seanfhocail na Mumhan* (Proverbs of Munster); new edition edited by Pádraig Ua Maoileoin, An Gúm, Baile Átha Cliath (Dublin), 1984. The original was published in 1926.

Tomás S. Ó Máille, editor. *Sean-fhocla Chonnacht* (Proverbs of Connacht); Oifig an tSoláthair, Baile Átha Cliath (Dublin), Vol. 1 1948, Vol. 2 1952.

Énrí Ó Muirgheasa, editor. *Seanfhocail Uladh* (Proverbs of Ulster); new edition edited by Nollaig Ó hUrmoltaigh, Oifig an tSoláthair, Baile Átha Cliath (Dublin), 1976. The original was published in 1907.

Fireside and Candlelight

"What harm?" says Jerry when he burned the house.

A man's house is his castle.
Is fearr bothán 's bainne gabhair agat féin, ná caisleán ag duine eile. [C]
Your own shack with goat's milk is better than someone else's castle.

It's a poor house that can't keep one lady.

Keep your house and your house will keep you.
Coinnigh do shiopa is coinneoidh do shiopa thú. [C]
Keep your shop and your shop will keep you.

A house divided will soon fall.
An áit a mbíonn i bpáirt, bíonn a leath ar lár. [C]
Half of the place which is divided will fall.

It is easier to knock a house than to build one.
["To knock" means "to knock down" or "to demolish."]

There can be no window where there is no wall.

There's no corner like one's own corner.

There is no hearthstone like your own hearthstone.
Níl aon teallach mar do theallach féin.
[The open fire was at floor level on a flag or hearthstone.]

Home sweet home and the fire out.
Ní teach teach gan teine. [C]
A house without a fire is not a home.

Bare walls make giddy housekeepers.
Ballaí fuara a níos bean tí suarach. [C]
Bare walls make a giddy housekeeper.

A red chimney, a hot house.

When everybody's house is on fire, go home and look at your own chimney.
Nuair atá teach do chomharsan le thine tabhair aire do do theach féin. [U]
When your neighbor's house is on fire, take care of your own house.

It is easier to build two chimneys than to keep smoke in one.

It takes a dirty hand to make a clean hearth.
Ní féidir im a bheith agam gan bláthach. [C]
I cannot have butter without buttermilk.

It is easy to kindle a fire on an old hearth.
It is never hard to light a half-burned turf.
Is furas aibhleog a fhadú. [U]
It is easy to light an ember.
[Turf or peat is the fossil fuel from bogland and it was once extensively used.]

A spark may raise an awful blaze.
Is beag an aithinne a dhéanfadh dó. [C]

Kindle the dry sticks and the green ones will catch.

Little sticks kindle a fire, great ones put it out.

Ash green makes a fire for the queen.
[Ash green would be fresh, unseasoned ash wood.]

A little fire to warm you is better than a great one to harm you.
Is fearr tine bheag a ghoras ná tine mhór a loisceas. [U]
A little fire that warms is better than a great fire that burns.

Don't burn your fingers when you have a tongs.

Silk stockings and burned shins.
Stocaí bána ar loirgne breaca. [C]
White stockings on speckled shins.

The hag is the better of being warmed but she is worse of being burned.
Is fearrde dhon chailleach a goradh, ach is miste dhi í a loscadh. [C]

It's often the ashy pet put out the man that makes the stack.
Chuir fear na luatha fear na cruaiche amach. [M]
It's often the man of the ashes put the man of the stacks out.
[The stack is the turfstack that is positioned adjacent to the house on the sheltered side.]

"More light," said the hag when the house was on fire.
"More light," ars an chailleach nuair a bhí an teach le thine. [U]

Never burn a penny candle looking for a halfpenny.

When you burn the candle you can burn the butt.
Burn the candle and burn the inch.
Nuair a chaith tú an choinneal, caith an t-orlach. [U]
When you have burnt the candle, burn the inch.

When the two ends are alight the candle does not burn long.
Nuair atá dhá thaobh na coinnle lasta, cha seasann sí i bhfad. [U]
When the two ends of the candle are alight it does not last long.

The man in the moon wants no peeled rushes.
[Peeled rushes were used in the making of rushlights. Rushes were stripped to expose the pith which was then dried and dipped in melted fat to form slender candles.]

Dull tins, lazy housekeeper.

Sweep the corners—the middle will sweep itself.

A new broom is the dart.
Scuab nua is fearr a scuabas an t-urlár. [C]
A new broom is the best at sweeping the floor.
["Dart": best thing?]
A new broom sweeps clean but the old one knows the corners best.
Scuabann scuab úr go glan, ach tá fios ag an seanscuab ar na coirnéil. [U]
A new broom sweeps clean but the old broom knows the corners.

Sit on your heels till the stool is footed.
Ná suigh ar an stól go mbí sé formáilte fút. [C]
Do not sit on the stool until it is stable under you.
["Footed" is "made."]

Don't break your laidhricín on a stool that isn't in your way.
Ná bris do loirgín ar stól nach bhfuil in do shlí. [U]
Don't break your shin on a stool that isn't in your way.
["Laidhricín" is "little toe." The proverb was collected in County Sligo.]

You can't make a mahogany table out of a whin bush.
[Whin (*Ulex* species) is a common species with thin, gnarled branches.]
You can't make a piano out of a bacon box.

Never bolt your door with a boiled carrot.

Many feathers make a bed.
Líontar sac le póiríní. [C]
A sack can be filled (even) with small potatoes.

There is no place like the bed!
Níl áit ar bith mar an baile. [C]
There is no place like home.

He's a very drunk man that would fall out of a settle bed.
[A settle bed was the forerunner of the bed-settee. When it was opened out into a bed, it had high, box-like sides.]

The drop follows the scollop.
[In heavy rain, the water often ran in along the scollops—the sally, that is, willow rods which were used in many areas to secure the roof thatch. The proverb has been used to describe how a certain family characteristic will descend through several generations.]

A windy day is not the day for the scollops.
Chan é lá na gaoithe lá na scolbach. [U]

It's useless cutting scallops when the wind rises.
It is too late to point the scallops when the wind rises.

An empty house needs no thatch.
Scioból folamh, cha bhíonn díon de dhíth air. [U]
An empty barn needs no roof.

It is a lonesome street without a cart.
Is uaigneach an rud teach folamh. [C]
An empty house is a lonesome thing.
[This proverb was collected in County Leitrim, an area where the word "street" can mean "farmyard."]

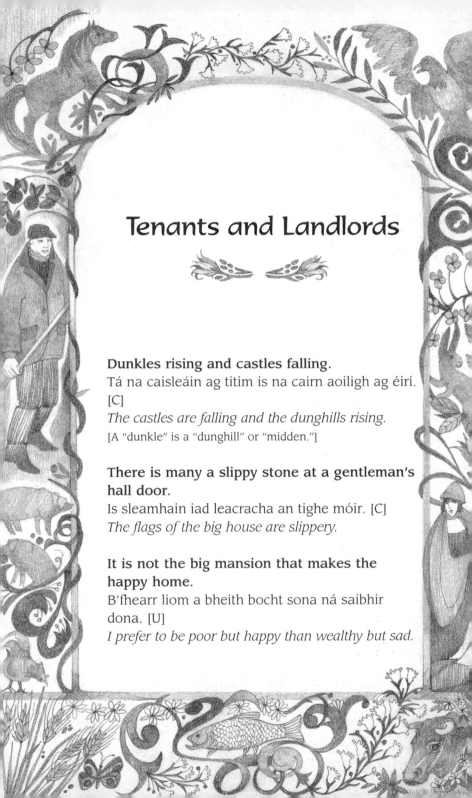

Tenants and Landlords

Dunkles rising and castles falling.
Tá na caisleáin ag titim is na cairn aoiligh ag éirí.
[C]
The castles are falling and the dunghills rising.
[A "dunkle" is a "dunghill" or "midden."]

There is many a slippy stone at a gentleman's hall door.
Is sleamhain iad leacracha an tighe móir. [C]
The flags of the big house are slippery.

It is not the big mansion that makes the happy home.
B'fhearr liom a bheith bocht sona ná saibhir dona. [U]
I prefer to be poor but happy than wealthy but sad.

An empty house is better than a bad tenant.
Is fearr teach folamh ná drochthionónta. [U]

Cleaning the house will not pay the rent.
Ní teach glan a íocfas cíos. [C]
A clean house will not pay rent.

Rent for the landlord or food for the children.
Cíos do thiarna nó bia do linbh. [C]

Said when someone was having difficulty in apportioning money and also found in this even more forthright form:

Your lord's rent or your child's life.

Many a baron wore a bawneen.
["Bawneen" is from the Irish "báinín," undyed, homespun woolen cloth.]

Three removes are worse than an eviction.
"Removing" or "flitting" was generally not approved of. This is an adaptation of the more widely known proverb that refers to fires:
Two removes are as bad as a burning.
Cha bhíonn imirce gan chaill. [U]
There is no removal without loss.

Pay Leitrim the rent and you're safe.
[This was collected in County Leitrim, the Lords Leitrim having been major landlords there.]

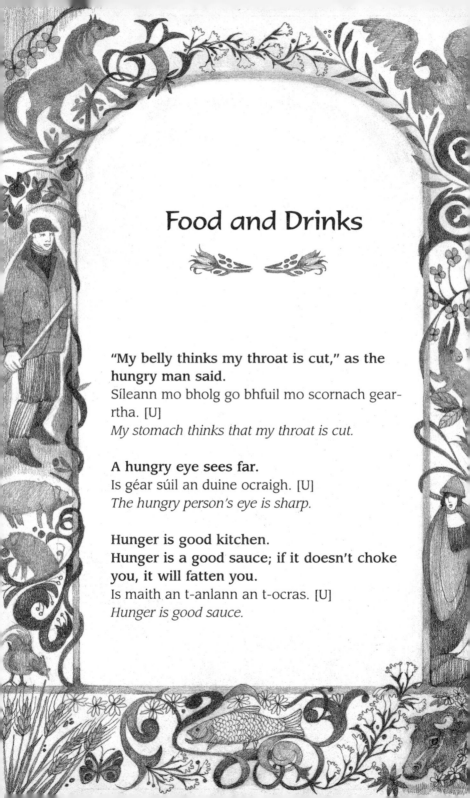

Food and Drinks

"My belly thinks my throat is cut," as the hungry man said.
Síleann mo bholg go bhfuil mo scornach gear-rtha. [U]
My stomach thinks that my throat is cut.

A hungry eye sees far.
Is géar súil an duine ocraigh. [U]
The hungry person's eye is sharp.

Hunger is good kitchen.
Hunger is a good sauce; if it doesn't choke you, it will fatten you.
Is maith an t-anlann an t-ocras. [U]
Hunger is good sauce.

Hunger will conquer a lion.
Brisfidh an t-ocras fríd bhalla cloch. [U]
Hunger will break through a stone wall.

It is a good thing to be hungry when you have something to eat.

Where there is a gant there is a want (for either meat, money, or drink).
[A "gant" is a "yawn."]

Talk doesn't fill the stomach.
Cha líontar an bolg le caint. [U]

As is the cook so is the kitchen.

A blunt knife shows a bad housekeeper.

A good fire makes a speedy cook.
Ní tine mhaith cócaire tapaidh. [U]

What won't choke will fatten and clean dirt is no poison.

The worst at work is first at the table.
Fear ag an bhia is dearóil san obair. [U]
A man at food and feeble at work.

Last to the work, first to the table.
Tús ag an phota is deireadh ag an obair. [U]
First at the pot and last at the work.

Help is always welcome except at the table.
Is maith an rud cúnamh, ach ag an mbord. [C]
Help is a good thing except at the table.

Easy to be flaithiúil with another person's share.
Nach flaithiúil atá tú fá chuid do chomharsan? [C]
Aren't you generous with what belongs to your neighbor?
["Flaithiúil" is "generous."]

Don't put in your cutty among spoons.
Ná cuir do ladar i meadar gan iarraidh. [C]
Don't put your ladle into the mether without being invited.
[In other words, do not meddle or interfere. "Cutty" here is a short-handled horn or wooden spoon while a "mether" is a four-sided wooden vessel.]

You don't know what is in the pot till the lid is lifted.
Pota bruith-mhagaidh agus clár air. [C]
A mock-boiling pot with its lid on.
Fan go bhfeicidh tú cad é tá sa bpota. [C]
Wait until you see what is in the pot.

Cool before you sup.
Fuaraigh sula n-óla tú. [U]

A little tastes sweet.
Bíonn blas ar an bheagán. [U]

A fat kitchen never leaves a lean will.

A fat kitchen makes a lean purse.

A full stomach never thinks of an empty one.
Ní airíonn an té atá sách bolg seang. [C]
The sated person does not notice the empty stomach.

Don't leave a tailor's remnant behind you.
Ná fág fuíollach táilliúir in do dhiaidh. [U]

Scant feeding to man or horse is a small profit and sure loss.

He sups ill, who eats all at dinner.
[Dinner is the meal at midday, which was usually the most substantial one of the day.]

One without dinner means two for supper.
Duine gan dinnéar beirt chun suipéir. [M]

BUTTER AND BUTTER MAKING

Before creameries became widespread, every house had its churn, and in season butter making was practically an everyday activity. Good butter was prized and what was not needed at home could be marketed.

A running cow's milk is hard to churn.

Long churning makes bad butter.
Maistreadh fada a níos an drochim. [U]
The longer the churning the tougher the butter.
A long churning makes bad butter, but be sure and have the churn scrubbed.

The more water the less butter.

Some people, when they get their heads above the churn, would not drink buttermilk.
Is beag orm bláthach nuair bhím lán di. [C]
Buttermilk means little to me when I am full of it.

Winded butter tastes bad.
["Winded" is spoiled or tainted by exposure to air; rancid.]

Yellow butter sells best.

The person who has butter gets more butter.
Té a bhfuil im aige gheibh sé im. [U]
The one who has butter will get butter.

Butter won't choke a dog.
Is iomdha caoi le cat a thachtadh seachas a thachtadh le him. [C]
There are many ways of choking a cat besides choking it with butter.

Don't buy butter for cats to lick.

It's dear-bought butter that's licked off a briar.
An té arb' annsa leis mil as neantóig, íocann sé rádhaor as. [C]
The person who loves honey from nettles pays too dearly for it.
[A briar is the thorny branch of the bramble bush.]

Butter to butter is no kitchen.
Im le him chan tarsann é. [U]
["Kitchen" is "relish"—a little dab of something well-flavored added to plain fare to make it more appetizing. This has been used when two men are seen dancing together or when two women kiss.]

Champ to champ will choke you.
["Champ" is a name used in northern parts of the island for mashed potatoes.]

Never put the butter through the porridge.
The butter will burst through the stirabout.
["Stirabout" is an alternative name for porridge.]
The butter went through the colcannon on him.
D'imigh an t-im tríd an chál cheannann air. [U]
[His plans miscarried. Colcannon was a popular dish of mashed potato mixed with chopped vegetables, such as cabbage and onion. It is now enjoying a revival in some restaurants.]

MEAL, PORRIDGE, AND BREAD

If you don't save at the cord you can't do it at the bottom.
Ní i dtóin an mhála, ach i dtosach an mhála, is cóir tíos a dhéanamh. [C]
Management should be not at the bottom of the sack but at the top.
Always going to the chest and never putting in soon brings the meal to the bottom.
[Meal was often stored in a wooden chest.]

You can't make stirabout without meal.
Cha dtig leat leite a dhéanamh gan min. [U]
It's hard to make stirabout without meal.
Is deacair brachán a dhéanamh gan min. [C]

Half and half makes good porridge.
[That is, a mixture of half oats to half imported maize or "Indian meal," as it was called. At one time oats were so dear to buy that they were mixed with the cheaper Indian meal to make them go further.]

There is skill in all things, even in making porridge.
Le stuaim a baintear báirneach. [C]
Limpets are (only) obtained through skill.
Tá stuaim ar ithe na mine. [C]
There is skill in eating meal.

Nature binds the meal to the potstick.

Where there's meal there is surely salt.

Don't put in your spoon where there is no porridge.

Don't scald your lips with another man's porridge.

It is easy to bake beside the meal.
Is furas fuineadh in aice mine. [U]

A man who has a loaf will get a knife to cut it.
An té a bhfuil builín aige, gheobhaidh sé scian a ghearrfas é.
[C]

A slice off half a loaf is not missed.

Crooked bread makes straight bellies.
Ní arán cam bolg díreach. [U]
Crooked bread makes a straight belly.

Raw dods make fat lads.
[A dod is a lump of bread.]

BROTH, MEAT, FISH, AND VEGETABLES

You cannot sup soup with a fork.
Níl ann ach seafóid a bheith ag ól anraithe le forc. [C]
It is only nonsense to be drinking soup with a fork.

The second boiled broth is always the best.

A stew boiled is a stew spoiled.

Keep your heart up for frettin's but bad kitchen to your meat.
Coinnigh suas do chroí, beidh aimsir mhaith againn go sea.
[U]
Keep your heart up, we will have good weather yet.

A bit of a rabbit is worth two bits of a cat.
Is fearr greim de choinín ná dhá ghreim de chat. [U]
One bite of a rabbit is better than two bites of a cat.

"Just to have it to say," said the old man who ate the bit of the dog.

A pig's ear can never make mutton.
Ní bheith tú ábalta sparán síoda a dhéanamh as cluais muice. [U]
You will not be able to make a silk purse of a pig's ear.

Don't pluck your goose until you catch her.
Ná haltaigh do bhia go mbeidh sé i do mhála. [C]
Don't give thanks for your food until it is in your bag.

The younger the chicken the sweeter the picking.

Chicken today and feathers tomorrow.

An egg today is better than a roasted ox tomorrow.
Is fearr ubh indiu ná damh i mbárach. [C]
An egg today is better than an ox tomorrow.

Better is a small fish than an empty dish.
Is fearr aon fhata amháin ná lán pláta dhe chraicne. [C]
One single potato is better than a plateful of skins.

A good apple-eater is a bad sharer.

Some likes an apple and some likes an onion.

The old man to the big potato.

Better have potatoes and salt—and peace.

MILK AND TEA, WATER, WINE, AND PORTER

The juice of a cow is good alive or dead.
Is maith sú bó, beo nó marbh. [U]

No cure for spilled milk, only lick the pitcher.
Níl aon fháil ar an mbainne a doirtear. [C]
There is no recouping spilled milk.

Don't skim the top off the milk before you send it to the creamery.

Tea seldom spoils when water boils.

Dead with tea and dead without it.
Marbh le tae agus marbh gan é. [U]

There is nothing as mean as tea in a tin.

He who only drinks water does not get drunk.
An té a ólas ach uisce, cha bhíonn sé ar meisce. [U]

Water is a good drink if taken in the right spirit.

Wine today, water tomorrow.
Fíon indiu, uisce amárach. [C]

Wine drowns more men than water.

Wine is sweet but the results are bitter.
Dá fheabhas an t-ól, 'sé an tart a dheireadh. [C]
However pleasant the drink, it always ends in thirst.

The three faults of drink is:
a sorrowful morning,
a dirty coat,
and an empty pocket.
Trí bhua an ólacháin:
maidin bhrónach,
cóta salach,
pócaí folamha. [C]
The three results of drink:...

The drunkard will soon have daylight in through the rafters.
An té a leanas ól, chan fada go dtiocfaidh solas an lae
isteach ar mhullach an toighe. [U]
The follower of drink will soon have daylight coming in through
the roof of the house.

Except you are drinking never lean against a public house.
Ach mur' mbeidh tú ag ól, ná bí ag cuimil do dhroma don toigh leanna. [U]

You'll never miss the porter until the barrel runs dry.
A parody of the more widely known:
You'll never miss the water till the well runs dry.
Chan fhuil meas ar an uisce go dtriomáithear an tobar. [U]
Water is not valued until the well dries up.
[Porter is a dark beer or stout that is still very popular.]

Empty kettles never leak.

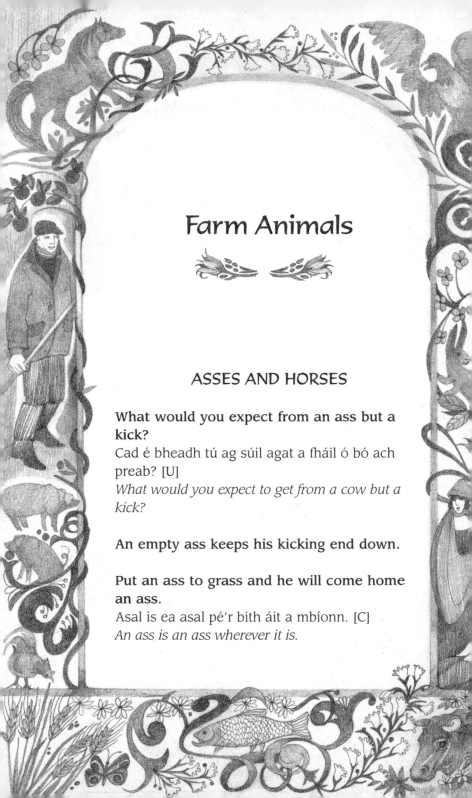

Farm Animals

ASSES AND HORSES

What would you expect from an ass but a kick?
Cad é bheadh tú ag súil agat a fháil ó bó ach preab? [U]
What would you expect to get from a cow but a kick?

An empty ass keeps his kicking end down.

Put an ass to grass and he will come home an ass.
Asal is ea asal pé'r bith áit a mbíonn. [C]
An ass is an ass wherever it is.

An ass never goes bald.

I cannot whistle, chew meal, and drive an ass.
Cha dtig le duine feadalaigh agus min a chogaint. [U]
A person cannot whistle and chew meal.
Ní féidir bheith a' seoladh na mbó 's dá mbleaghan. [U]
It is not possible to be driving the cows and milking them.

Slow but sure like Murphy's ass.

Better is an ass that carries you than a horse that throws you.
Is fearr asal a iomchras thú ná capall a chaitheas thú. [U]

A whip for the horse, a bridle for the donkey, and a rod for the fool's back.
Bó le bata is capall le ceansacht. [M]
A cow with a stick and a horse with gentleness.
[To guide them.]

What can you expect from a cob but a kick?

Better a poor horse in an empty stall, better half a loaf than none at all.
Is fearr caora bhearrtha ná dhá chaorigh gan fáirnéis. [C]
One shorn sheep is better than two sheep without trace.
Is fearr leathbhuilín ná bheith folamh ar fad. [U]
Half a loaf is better than to have nothing at all.

Those who would slight my horse would buy my horse.
An fear a cháineas mo ghearrán, ceannóidh sé mo ghearrán. [U]
The man who slights my horse will buy my horse.

You can't judge a horse by his harness.
Ná tóg leabhar lena chlúdach. [C]
Don't take a book by its cover.

Saddle the right horse.
Cuir an diallait ar an chapall cheart. [U]

Some for the saddle and more for the straddle.
[Some for lighter work than others. A straddle is a pack saddle from which carrying baskets called "panniers" were hung. It was once widely used on both horses and donkeys.]

A gray horse looks well in a bog.
Is furas gearrán bán a fheiceáil ar an chorrach. [U]
It is easy to see a white horse on the bog.

The best horse jumps the ditch.
An capall is fearr, léimfidh sé an claí. [U]

He's a good horse that pulls his own load.
Is maith an capall a tharraingeos a hualach féin. [C]

It is a proud horse won't carry his own corn.
Gan fhónamh an capall nach n-iompródh a choirce féin. [U]
The horse that won't carry its own oats is useless.
["Corn" is the common name for "oats."]

An eating horse won't founder.

An old horse needs fresh grass.

It's hard to put an old horse from kicking.
Is deacair falaireacht a bhaint as seanchapall. [U]
It's hard to stop an old horse from ambling.

A borrowed horse has hard hooves, or has no soul.
Bíonn cosa cruaidh ag gearrán iasacht'. [U]

It is easy to drive with your own whip and another's horse.
Do fhuip féin is capall na comharsan. [C]
Your own whip and the neighbor's horse.
Do spoir féin is capall duine eile. [M]
Your own spurs and another's horse.

COWS

"Every man to his fancy, and me to my own Nancy," said the old woman when she kissed her cow.

The man of the cow in the tail.
Fear na bó 'san ruball. [U]
[At its assistance.]

The worst cow in the bawn bawls first.
Sí an bhó is salaí iorball an bhó is airde géim. [C]
The cow with the dirtiest tail lows loudest.
[A "bawn" is a cattle-fold.]

The taste of the clover makes a thief of the cow.

**The old cow for
the sour grass.**
["Sour grass" is "coarse
grass."]

**From her head the
cow is milked.**
Is as a ceann a
bhlítear an bhó.
[U]

**A starved cow
never fills the pail.**

I'd far rather the cow that would give the full of a thimble than the one that would give the full of a churn and spill it.
B'fhearr gabhar nach dtabharfadh ach lán méaragáin ná bó a bhéarfadh lán na cuinneoige is a dhoirtfeadh. [U]
Better a goat that only gives a thimbleful of milk than a cow that gives a churnful and spills it.
What is the use of a good cow when she spills her milk?
Cé'n mhaith bó mhaith, dá ndoirteadh sí a cuid bainne? [U]

Modest maoly the biggest devil in the byre.
An mhart mhodhúil mhaol an mhart is crosta i dteach na mbó. [U]
The modest, hornless beast, the crossest cow in the byre.
[Maoly cattle are a hornless breed peculiar to Ireland; only a small number still exist. The proverb may be referring to this type, or simply to a dehorned cow.]

A bad cow is better than none.
Is fearr buaile seasc ná buaile folamh. [M]
A dry booley is better than an empty booley.
[A booley is a temporary milking place while on summer pasture. A dry booley would be one where the cows are not giving milk.]

A heifer's heifer fills the byre.

There are long horns on the cows in Connacht.
Tá adharca fada ar bhuaibh i gConnachta. [U]
Kerry cows have long horns.
Cows in Meath have long horns.
Cows across the sea have long horns.
Bíonn adharca fada ar na ba thar lear. [C]
Far away cows have long horns but they often come home mileys.
["Miley" is the same as "maoly"; see above. The English-language versions above all came from County Cavan.]

SHEEP AND GOATS

Tethered sheep will not thrive.

Do not lose the sheep for a halfpenny worth of tar.
Ná caill an chaora fá luach leithphingine tharra. [U]

Every scabby sheep likes a comrade.
Cha raibh caora chlamhach ar an tréad riamh nár mhaith léi
comrádaí a bheith aici. [U]
*There never was a scabby sheep in the flock that did not like to
have a companion with her.*

One scabby sheep spoils a whole flock.
Salachaidh aon chaora chlamhach sréad. [U]

**If one sheep puts his head through the gap the rest will
follow.**
An rud a níos gabhar déanfaidh gabhar eile é. [C]
What one goat does another goat will do.
Nuair a chacann gé cacann siad go léir. [C]
When one goose defecates they all defecate.
Nuair a luíonn gé luíonn siad go léir. [C]
When one goose lies down they all lie down.

Like and alike is a bad mark among sheep.
Cosúil le chéile—sin drochmharc i measc na gcaorach. [U]
Like one another—that is a bad mark amongst sheep.

Don't go putting wool on the sheep's back.
Is dona an rud an iomarca saille a chur ar dhroim muice
beathaithe. [C]
It's a bad thing to put too much fat on a well-fed pig's back.

"You're a devil, my dear," says Ned Ennis to the goat.

**When you see a goat you should always hit him because
he is either going into mischief or coming out of it.**

When the goat goes to the door of the chapel she will not stop until she goes to the altar.
Nuair a théann an gabhar 'on teampall ní stadann go haltóir. [M]
When the goat goes to the church it does not stop until the altar.

If you put a silk suit on a goat it is still a goat.
Cuir síoda ar gabhar is is gabhar i gcónaí é. [U]
Put silk on a goat and it is still a goat.

It is difficult to cut wool off a goat.
Is doiligh olann a bhaint de ghabhar. [U]

Riding on a goat is better than the best of walking.
Is fearr marcaíocht ar ghabhar ná coisíocht ar fheabhas. [U]

PIGS

A full pig in the sty doesn't find the hungry one going by.
Ní aithníonn an mhuc a bhíos sa chró an mhuc a bhíos ag dul an ród. [U]
The pig in the sty does not acknowledge the pig on the road.

It's a young pig that wouldn't hoke.
["To hoke" means "to root."]

Keep your mind to yourself like a bonive.
[A "bonive" is an immature pig.]

It is not the big sow that eats the most.
Na muca ciúine a itheann an mhin. [M]
It is the quiet pigs that eat the meal.

Pigs won't thrive on clean water.

The thieving pig's ear can hear the grass growing.
Éisteacht na muice bradaí. [U]
The hearing of the thieving pig.
D'aireodh sé an féar ag fás. [M]
He would notice the grass growing.
["A thieving pig," one eating what it shouldn't, is supposed to have a keen sense of hearing.]

DOGS AND CATS

What could you expect from a dog but a bite?
Céard a bheadh súil agat cloisteáil ó mhuic ach gnúsacht? [C]
What would you expect to hear from a pig but a grunt?

You cannot trust a cur.

Idle dogs worry sheep.

For a mischievious dog a heavy clog.

Throw a bad dog a bone, a good dog won't bite you.
Caith an cnámh chuig an drochmhada 's ní baol duit an deamhada. [C]
Throw the bone to the bad dog and the good dog won't be a danger to you.

A well-bred dog goes out when he sees them preparing to kick him out.

It's hard to make a choice between two blind dogs.
Is deacair rogha a bhaint as dhá ghabhar chaocha. [M]
It's hard to make a choice between two blind goats.

The dog is teann at his own door.
Is teann an madadh ar a thairseach féin. [U]
The dog is teann on his own threshold.
["Teann," from the Irish, means "bold."]

A dog with two homes is never any good.

Don't let your bone go with the dog.
Ná lig do chnámh leis an mada. [C]

Keep the bone and the dog will follow.
Coinnigh an cnámh agus leanfaidh an madadh thú. [U]
Keep the bone and the dog will follow you.

The dog that fetches will carry.

Every dog has its duties.

Every dog has his day and some have two.

The old dog for the hard road and the pup for the boithrin.
An seanmhada dhon bhealach fada, is an coileán le haghaidh an bhóithrín. [C]
The old dog for the long way and the pup for the boithrin.
[A "boithrin," more often rendered "boreen," comes from the Irish "bóithrín," meaning a minor road or lane.]

It's hard to knock an old dog off his track.
Is deacair an mada a bhaint den tseanchasán. [C]
It's hard to make the dog leave the old path.
["To knock off" means "to divert from."]

An old dog cannot alter his way of barking.
An faisiún atá sa láimh, is deacair a bhaint aisti. [C]
The habit in the hand is difficult to eradicate.

To steal an old dog never try; you'll find your mistake by and by.

It's hard to teach an old dog to dance.
Is deacair damhsa a chur roimh sheanmhadaidh. [U]

You should not throw stones at a dead dog.
Caitheamh cloch ar mhadadh marbh. [U]
Throwing stones at a dead dog.

A dead dog will not bark.
Ní thig le mála falamh seasamh, ná le cat marbh siubhal. [C]
An empty sack cannot stand nor can a dead cat walk.

If the cat scrapes you don't beat the dog.

"I saw you before," says the cat to the boiling water.
"Chonac cheana thú," mar a dúirt an cat leis an mbainne beirithe. [M]
"I saw you before," as the cat said to the boiled milk.

Would a cat drink sweet milk?
An maith leis an gcat bainne leamhnachta? [U]
Does the cat like sweet milk?
[Sweet milk is whole, full cream milk as opposed to buttermilk, which is separated and sour.]

If the cat was churning it is often she would have her paws in it.
Dá mbeadh cuigeann ag an gcat ba mhinic a lapa féin ann. [M]

A wise cat never burned herself.
Níor dhóigh seanchat riamh é féin. [M]
An old cat never burnt itself.

One jump in the fire never burnt the cat.

What the good wife spares the cat eats.
An rud a choigleas na mná, itheann an cat é. [U]
What the women spare the cat eats.

Too many cats are worse than rats.

If the cat sits long enough at the hole she will catch the mouse.

When the cat is out the mouse can dance.
Nuair bhíos an cat amuigh, bíonn cead rince ag na luchóga. [C]
When the cat is out the mice can dance.

The cat's one shift is worth all the fox's.

[A "shift" means a "strategm." The cat's one shift is its ability to climb trees, something that the fox, despite its cleverness, can't do. This proverb may allude to the well-known international folktale *The Cat's Only Trick* (classified as AT105) in which the cat is able to escape from hunters up a tree while the fox left below on the ground is killed.]

The cat has leave to look at the queen and the queen has leave to shoot it.

Tá cead ag an gcat breathnú ar an mbanríon. [C]
The cat has leave to look at the queen.
Tá cead ag an gcat breathnú ar an rí, is tá cead ag an rí é a chaitheamh. [C]
The cat has leave to look at the king and the king has leave to shoot it.

A cat purrs for himself.

Is dó féin a ghníos an cat crónán. [C]
It is for its own good that the cat purrs.

It isn't for nothing the cat winks when she shuts both her eyes.

Ní gan ábhar a théas na caoirigh chuig an abhainn. [C]
It isn't without a reason the sheep go to the river.

Nature shines through the cat's eyes.

Briseann an dúchas trí shúile an chait. [U]
Nature breaks through the cat's eyes.

What's in the cat is in the kitten.

An rud atá sa gcat, tá sé ina pisín. [C]

Cat after kind makes a good mouser.

Gach cat i ndiaidh a chineáil. [U]
Every cat after its kind.

HENS, GEESE, AND DUCKS

Where you see shells you may guess eggs.
Thomhaisfeá uibheacha san áit a bhfeicfeá blaoscracha. [C]

It is a bad hen can't scrape for herself.
Is olc an chearc nach scríobann di féin. [U]

A laying hen is better than a nest of eggs.
Is fearr ceann indiu ná péire i mbárach. [C]
One today is better than two tomorrow.

The sitting hen never fattens.
Níor ramhraigh cearc ghoir riamh. [M]
[A "sitting hen" is one that is clocking or sitting on eggs to hatch them.]

The wisest hen at all lays out at times.
Is maith an chearc ná beireann amuigh. [M]
It is a good hen that does not lay out.

Though the hen may lay out, her eggs will be found.

You can't expect a big egg from a little hen.

It is not the hen that cackles most lays the largest egg.
Torann mór ar bheagán olann. [U]
A great noise for a little wool.

A dead hen is done laying.

The cocks crow
but the hens deliv-
er the goods.

Every cock can
crow on his own
dunghill.
Is teann gach
coileach ar a charn
aoiligh féin. [C]
*Every cock is bold on
its own dunghill.*

A dead cock never
crews.
Níl fear marbh a' dul ag innsean aon scéil. [C]
A dead man is not going to tell any tale.

If you want to keep up the stock keep an old gander and
a young cock.
Tarbh dá óige ná stail dá shine. [C]
A bull, however young, or a stallion, however old.

"You are welcome out," as Pára Bán said to the gosling.
[Pára Bán is a nickname, Pára being a diminutive of Pádraig (the Irish for
Patrick). "Bán" means fair-haired. Perhaps the color of Pára Bán's hair
resembled the gosling's down.]

Those who have a goose will get a goose.
A variation on the commoner:
They who have much get more.
An té a bhfuil mórán aige, is é a gheibh. [U]
The one who has much will get more.

Send a goose to Hanover and she will come back a goose over.
Má chuireann tú gé go dtí an domhan teas, ní bheidh sí ina gandal ag teacht ar ais. [C]
If you send a goose to the southern world she won't be a gander when she comes back.

"Time enough" lost the ducks and easy walking got them.
"Am go leor" a chaill na tonnóga. [U]
It was "time enough" that lost the ducks.
"Time enough" lost the duck but patience brought her home.

It's natural for ducks to go barefoot.
Sé dúchas na lachan snámh. [C]
It's natural for the duck to swim.

BEES

Beekeeping on farms, traditionally in conical straw skeps, was once more common than today. Lore about bees included informing them if there was a death in the household.

A rambling bee brings home the honey.
Ní chruinníonn cloch reatha caonach, ach cruinníonn meach siúil mil. [C]
A rolling stone gathers no moss but a traveling bee gathers honey.

Old bees yield no honey.

A small bee makes a cow gad.
Is minic a bhain creabhar preab as capall. [C]
A horsefly often made a horse flinch.

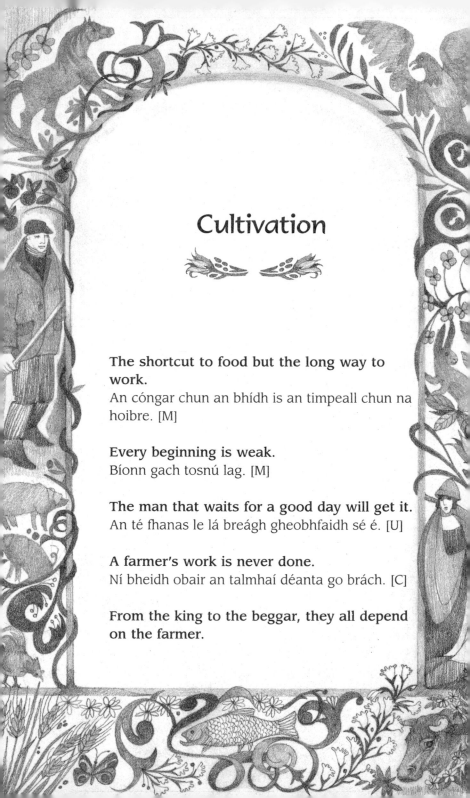

Cultivation

The shortcut to food but the long way to work.
An cóngar chun an bhídh is an timpeall chun na hoibre. [M]

Every beginning is weak.
Bíonn gach tosnú lag. [M]

The man that waits for a good day will get it.
An té fhanas le lá breágh gheobhfaidh sé é. [U]

A farmer's work is never done.
Ní bheidh obair an talmhaí déanta go brách. [C]

From the king to the beggar, they all depend on the farmer.

A good eye is worth two pairs of hands.
Is mó obair a níos súile an mháistir ná a chuid lámh. [C]
The eyes of the master do more work than his hands.

He who is a bad servant for himself is often a good servant for others.
An té bhíos ina dhrochsheirbhíseach dhó féin, is minic a bhíos sé ina sheirbhíseach mhaith do dhaoine eile. [C]

A backward man never prospers.
Ní gnáthach fear náireach éadálach. [M]
A reserved man does not usually prosper.
[A "backward" man is a reserved one.]

Work is better than talk.
Is fearr obair ná caint. [U]

Work while the bit is in your belly.

The more you tramp the dunghill the more the dirt rises.
Is leithne bualtrach bó le seasamh uirthi. [C]
Standing on cow dung spreads it out.

Sea-wrack on the strand never manures the land.
[In many coastal areas seaweed was used as a fertilizer.]

Put a mud turf on a dish and it will be a mud turf still.
[Mud turf is an inferior kind of turf needing more work to produce and not as efficient a fuel as the more solid spade-cut turf.]

The four worst things:
ploughing in frost,
harrowing in rain,
making a ditch in summer,
and building a wall in winter.
Treabhadh seaca is fuirseadh báistí, an dá rud is measa dhon talamh. [C]
Ploughing in frost and harrowing in rain, the two worst things for the ground.

It is not the day you are harrowing; you should feed your horse.
Ní hé lá na báistí lá an phortaigh. [C]
The rainy day is not the day for the bog.

The grass-harrow gathers no stones.

Harrowing is no good without cross-harrowing.

Have the supper ready when the harrow comes home.

You should never stop the plough to kill a mouse.

Seed must be saved before it's sown.

If you don't sow in the spring you will not reap in the autumn.
An té nach gcuireann san earrach, cha bhaineann sé san fhómhar. [U]
The one who doesn't sow in spring will not reap in autumn.

The seed you will sow is the corn you will reap.
Plant poacheens and you'll dig poacheens.
Má chuireann tú póiríní bainfidh tú póiríní. [C]
If you set small potatoes you will harvest small potatoes.
["Poacheens" are small potatoes.]

More grows in a tilled field than is sowed in it.
Fásann níos mó sa ngarraí ná cuirtear ann. [C]
More grows in the garden than is sowed in it.

Thistle seeds fly.

Time will tell and frost will dry the praties.
Neosaidh an aimsir. [C]
Time will tell.
["Praties" is a coloquial word for potatoes.]

If the potato misses Ireland's beaten.

Slight my meadow, buy my hay.
Más beag ort an léana, ná ceannaigh an féar. [U]
If you think little of the meadow do not buy the grass.

Time used sharpening a scythe is not time wasted.
Ní moill faobhar. [C]
Making a keen edge is not a holdup.

A good farmer is known by his crops.

It is not the big farmers who reap all the harvest.
Ní hiad na fir mhóra a ghearras an fómhar uilig. [C]
It is not the big men who reap all the harvest.

It is hard to get a good hook for a bad harvestman.
Is doiligh corrán maith a fháil do dhrochbhuanaí. [U]
[A "hook" is a reaping hook or sickle.]

"Time enough" never cut the barley.
"Tráth go leor," a chaill an rása. [C]
It was "Time enough" that lost the race.

Wisps make a bundle.
Níonn brobh beart. [C]
Bailíonn brobh beart (agus do-níd birt stáca). [M]
Every wisp swells the bundle (and bundles up make a stack).

APPLES AND ORCHARDS

No use in throwing apples into an orchard.
Ag caitheamh úll isteach san úllghort. [C]
Throwing apples into the orchard.
Don't throw apples into an orchard or carry turf to a bog.
Ag tabhairt cnó dho choll. [C]
Taking nuts to the hazel tree.
[Indigenous hazelnuts were an important protein source.]

Many a rose-cheeked apple is rotten at the core.
Is minic a bhíos an t-úll dearg go holc ina chroí. [C]
The red apple often has a vile core.

The shakiest tree in the orchard is sometimes the last to fall.
Chan é an crann a bhíos i bhfad ag crith an chéad chrann a thitfeas. [U]
It is not the tree that is shaking for a long time that will be the first tree to fall.

Little apples will grow big.
Tagann fata mór as póirín. [C]
Big potatoes develop from little potatoes.

When the apple is ripe it will fall.
Nuair a bheas an t-úll aibí titfidh sé. [U]

Don't wait for apples, gather your own windfalls.

One rotten apple rots a bagful.
Milleann caora tréad. [C]
A single sheep will/can ruin a flock.
Cuireann madadh amháin madaidh an bhaile ag tafann. [U]
One dog will set all the dogs of the town barking.

Apples will grow again.
Fásfaidh úlla arís. [C]

The tree remains but not so the hand that put it.
Maireann an crann, ach ní mhaireann an lámh a chuir é. [C]

At the Mill

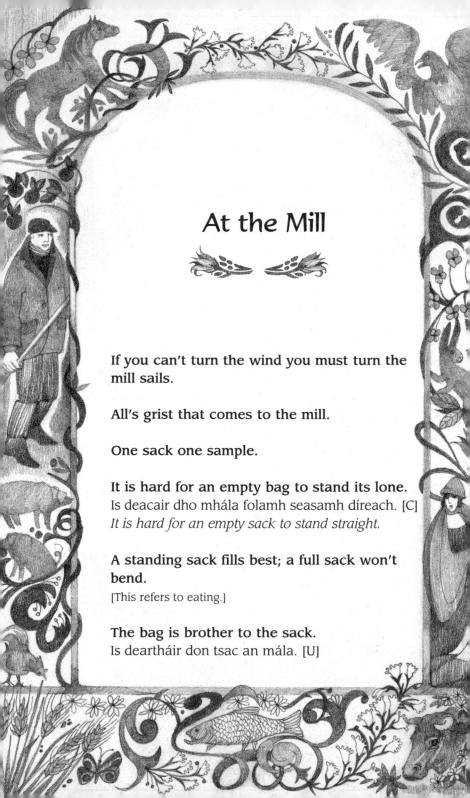

If you can't turn the wind you must turn the mill sails.

All's grist that comes to the mill.

One sack one sample.

It is hard for an empty bag to stand its lone.
Is deacair dho mhála folamh seasamh díreach. [C]
It is hard for an empty sack to stand straight.

A standing sack fills best; a full sack won't bend.
[This refers to eating.]

The bag is brother to the sack.
Is deartháir don tsac an mála. [U]

The miller's pigs are fat but it wasn't all mouter they ate.
Bíonn muca na muilteoirí ramhar; má tá, is ag Dia atá a fhios
cé leis an mhin a d'ith siad. [U]
*The miller's pigs are fat but, if they are, God knows whose meal
they ate.*
[Mouter was the portion of customers' grain that the miller kept in pay-
ment. In folk tradition the miller has a bad reputation and so the proverb
implies that the miller was keeping more than his due.]

If you don't want flour, do not go into the mill.
Mur' maith leat do mhéar a ghearradh, ná cuir roimh an
chorrán é. [U]
*If you don't want your finger cut, do not put it in front of the
reaping hook.*

Hunting and Fishing

"So near and yet so far," says the man when the bird lit on his gun.

A flying bird is any man's shot.

The wise bird flies lowest.

A closed fist never caught a bird.
Char ghabh dorn druidte seabhac riamh. [U]
A closed fist never caught a hawk.

An old fox is shy of a trap.
Cha gheabhthar seanéan le cáith. [U]
An old bird is not caught with chaff.

"We hounds kill the hare," quoth the lapdog.
Wee dogs start the hare but big ones catch her.
Cuirfidh an madadh beag an gearria ina shuí, ach caithfidh
an madadh mór a ghabháil. [U]
The small dog raises the hare but the big one has to catch it.

At times the slow hound is lucky.
Is minic cú mall sona. [M]
A slow hound is often lucky.

An old rogue is a good tracker.

It is hard to hunt the hare out of the bush it is not in.
Is doiligh an gearria a chur as an tomóg nach bhfuil sé ann.
[U]

Nearly never killed the hare.
Ní dhéanann "gearr dhó" an gnó. [C]
"Nearly" does not do the job.

First catch your hare and then cook it.
Ná maraigh an fia go bhfeicidh tú é. [C]
Do not kill the deer until you see it.

Long runs the hare but she is caught at last.
Más gasta an gearria beirtear fá dheireadh air.
Although the hare is speedy it will be caught at last.

Praise the sea but keep near land.
Mol an sliabh is ná taobhaigh í; cáin an tír is ná tréig í.
[M]
*Praise the mountain and do not approach it; dispraise the land
and do not abandon it.*

Don't make bold with the sea.
Ná déan dánaíocht ar an bhfarraige. [C]

**Listen to the sound of the river and you will catch a
trout.**
Éist le tuile na habhann is gheobhaidh tú breac. [U]
Listen to the flow of the river and you will catch a trout.
["Breac" can also mean any small fish.]

When you're not fishing be mending the nets.

**It's late to be mending your nets when the eels are in the
river.**
Is deireannach an t-ancoire
a chaitheamh amach nuair
tá an long ar charraig. [C]
*It's late to throw out the
anchor when the ship is on
the rock.*

**It's a good sign of fish to
see some in the nets.**
[This is used in retort to being
asked something obvious.]

It's seldom a fish loses his life for his breakfast.

A herring never was caught for his belly.
Mo ghrá-sa an scadán nár cailleadh ariamh lena ghoile! [C]
Good for (literally: "My love") the herring which was never lost
by its appetite!
[Herrings were netted rather than caught with bait.]

A herring in the pan is worth twenty in the sea.
Is fearr an breac atá sa dorn ná an breac atá san abhainn. [C]
The trout in the fist is better than the trout in the river.
A trout in the ashes is better than a salmon in the water.
Is fearr breac sa phota ná bradán sa linn. [U]
A trout in the pot is better than a salmon in the pool.

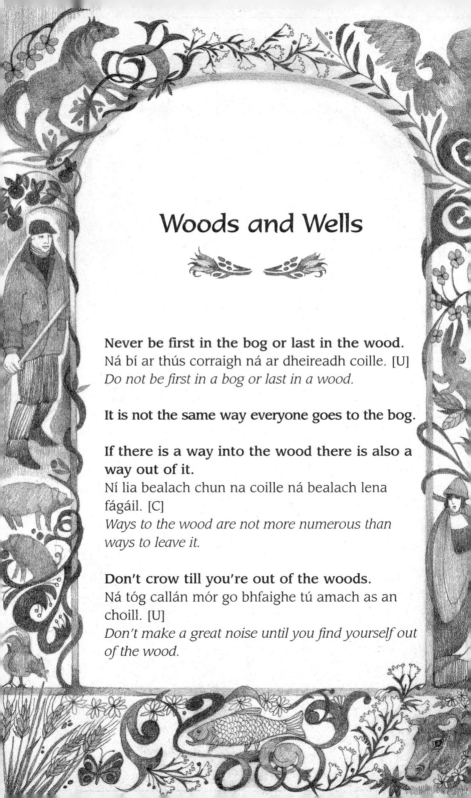

Woods and Wells

Never be first in the bog or last in the wood.
Ná bí ar thús corraigh ná ar dheireadh coille. [U]
Do not be first in a bog or last in a wood.

It is not the same way everyone goes to the bog.

If there is a way into the wood there is also a way out of it.
Ní lia bealach chun na coille ná bealach lena fágáil. [C]
Ways to the wood are not more numerous than ways to leave it.

Don't crow till you're out of the woods.
Ná tóg callán mór go bhfaighe tú amach as an choill. [U]
Don't make a great noise until you find yourself out of the wood.

There is no tree but has a branch rotten enough to burn.

You will find enough of brushna in every wood to burn it.

Tá a loscadh féin i ngach coill. [U]

In every wood is its own kindling.

["Brushna" is "kindling." This can be used to imply that there is a skeleton in the cupboard of every family.]

Bend with the tree that will bend with you.

Crom leis an chraobh a chromas leat. [U]

Bend with the branch that bends with you.

If the rowan tree is tall even so it is bitter on top.

Cé gurb ard é an crann caorthainn, bíonn sé searbh ar a bharr. [C]

[The rowan tree (*Sorbas aucuparia*) has stunning-looking but bitter-tasting orange-red berries.]

Little by little the oak tree grows.

Don't expect a cherry tree from an acorn.

Cha dtig ón driseog ach an sméar. [U]

*Nothing comes from the bramble (*Rubus fruticosus*) but the blackberry.*

An apple can't grow on a crab tree.

Ní féidir sméar a bhaint as sceach gheal. [C]

You can't get blackberries from a hawthorn.

The older the crab tree the more crabs it bears.

Willows are weak but they bind other wood.

"One look before is better than two behind," as the man said when he fell into the well.
Is fearr aon fhéachaint amháin romhat ná dhá fhéachaint id dhiaidh. [M]
One look in front of you is better than two looks behind you.

The deeper the well the better the water.

It's a pure spring that never runs dry.

If you break the ice it is easy lifting a bucket of water.

Cold water will scald a clart.
[A "clart" is a dirty, slovenly woman. The proverb was collected in County Monaghan.]

Never throw out the dirty water until you get in the clean.
Ná caith an t-uisce salach amach go dtabhra tú an t-uisce glan isteach. [U]
Do not throw out the dirty water until you bring in the clean water.

You never know the want of water till the well goes dry.
Níl fhios cén scáth atá sa tom go ngearrfar í. [C]
It is not realized what shelter a bush gives until it is cut.

Shallow brooks are noisy.
Is é an t-uisce is éadoimhne is mó tormán. [U]
Shallowest water is noisiest.

If you had the Shannon in hell you'd soon be a millionaire.
[The Shannon, a powerful river, is the longest in Ireland and flows south
from County Cavan into the sea at Limerick.]

Hills far away are green but they often have sour bottoms.
Is glas iad na cnoic i bhfad uainn, más glasmhar iad, ní
féarmhar. [C]
Hills far from us are green, but if they are, they are not grassy.
["Sour" here means "boggy and infertile."]

Wildlife

"Sour grapes," says the fox when he couldn't catch the chicken.

A sleeping fox catches no fowl.
Ní hé an sionnach a bhíos ina chodladh is mó a mharaíos éanlaith. [C]
The sleeping fox is not the one that kills most fowl.

"More beard than brains," as the fox said of the goat.
"Is faide do chuid féasóige ná do chuid intleachta," mar a dúirt an sionnach leis an ngabhar. [C]
"Your beard is more extensive than your intellect,"
as the fox said to the goat.

The fox never found a better messenger than himself.
Chan fhuair an madadh rua teachtaire riamh ab fhearr ná é
féin. [U]

The fox finds his own stink first.
Is é an madarua is túisce a fhaigheann boladh a bhroma féin. [M]
The fox notices the smell of its own fart first.

"Up and at it again," as the hedgehog said to the hare.
[This is a reference to the fable in which a slow animal, through trickery,
wins a race against a swift animal.]

The last kick of a dying rat is always the worst.

**Very few flocks that some bird out of them does not soil
its own nest.**
Ní bhíonn aon tréad gan raimín. [M]
There is no flock without its troublemaker.

Little by little the bird builds her nest.
I ndiaidh a chéile a thógtar na caisleáin. [U]
Little by little castles are built.

A crow won't caw without cause.
Ní gan fáth a dhéanas an searrach seitreach. [C]
It is not without a reason that the foal whinnies.

You can't teach a swallow how to fly.
An t-uan ag muineadh méilí dá mháthair. [M]
The lamb teaching its mother how to bleat.

A sandlark can't attend two strands.
Cha dtig leis an ghobadán friotháil ar an dá thrá. [U]
[A "sandlark" is probably the common sandpiper (*Tringa hypoleucos*).]

You can't check a snipe for having a long bill.
Ba dhual do lao an fhia rith a bheith aige. [U]
It is natural for a deer's fawn to have fleetness.

A wild goose never lays a tame egg.

A swan would die with pride only for its black feet.

The raven thinks her own young fair.
Is geal leis an bhfiach dubh a ghearrcach féin. [M]
The raven thinks her own nestling fair.

Every little frog is great in his own bog.
Is máistreas an luchóg ar a tigh féin. [U]
The mouse is mistress in her own house.

You can't pluck a frog.

Seven herrings are a meal for a salmon.
Seacht scadán díol bradáin,
Seacht mbradán díol róin,
Seacht róin díol muice mara,
Seacht muca mara díol míl mhóir,
Seacht míl mhóra díol an cheannruáin chróin,
Seacht gceannruáin chrón díol an domhain mhóir. [C]
Seven herrings are a meal for a salmon,
Seven salmon are a meal for a seal,
Seven seals are a meal for a porpoise,
Seven porpoises are a meal for a whale,
Seven whales are a meal for a smooth blenny,
Seven smooth blennies are a meal for an entire world.

"Strength," said the scutty wren when she pulled the maggot out of the hole.
"Neart," arsa an dreoilín nuair thit sé ar a thóin ag tarraingt péiste as an talamh. [C]
"Strength," said the wren when it fell on its rear pulling a worm out of the ground.

One beetle knows another.
Aithníonn ciaróg ciaróg eile. [U]

It's often a cleg made a bullock fart.
Is minic a bain cuileog léim as bulóg. [C]
A fly often made a bullock start.
[A cleg is a horsefly.]

Of small account is a fly till it gets into the eye.
Is beag le rá an chuileog nó go dté sí ins an tsúil. [C]

Highroads and Byroads

"I see," says the blind man when he was directed on his way.
"Chím," arsa an dall. "Thug tú t'éitheach," arsa an balbhán. [C]
"I see," said the blind man. "You're a liar," said the mute.

He who is bad for lodging is good for directing.
An té atá go dona fá lóistín, tá sé go maith fán tuairisc. [C]
The one who is bad for lodging is good for directing.

Ditches have ears.
Bíonn cluasa ar na claíocha. [C]
[Here a ditch is a raised boundary.]

Half a leap falls into the ditch.
An té nách bhfuil léim aige, leagann sé an claí. [C]
He who cannot jump demolishes the dyke.

Never cross the fields while you have the road to go.
Never take the byway when you have the highway.
Ná tréig an bóthar mór mar gheall ar an aichearra. [U]
Do not abandon the main road for the sake of a shortcut.

Be the road straight or crooked the high road is the shortest.
Cam nó díreach an ród, is é an bealach mór an aichearra. [U]

First-class walking is better than third-class riding.

A going foot will always light on something.
Gheibheann cos ar siúl rud éigin. [C]
A foot on the move will (always) find something.
A stirring foot always gets something even if it's only a thorn.
Faigheann cos siúl rud eicín, mara bhfaighidh sí ach dealg. [C]

No thorn as bad as the one out of the clabar.
["Clabar" is from the Irish "clabár," meaning "mud."]

A thorn,
a hound's tooth,
a fool's word.
[These are held to be the three sharpest things.]
Fiacal con,
dealg láibe,
nó focal amadáin:
ná trí nithe is géire amuigh. [M]
A hound's tooth,
a thorn in the mud,
or a fool's word:
the three sharpest things at all.

Never praise a ford till you are over.
Molann gach duine an t-ádh nuair fhághas sé é. [C]
Everyone praises the ford when he leaves it.

Leave the kiesh as it is.
Fág an Cheis mar tá sí. [C]
Leave Kesh as it is.
[A kesh is a causeway constructed across boggy ground. "Kesh"
occurs frequently in place-names—for example: Long Kesh, County
Antrim, Keshcarrigan, County Leitrim, and simply Kesh, County
Fermanagh.]

"Who knows?" as the woman said when she followed the
coach.

The loosest spoke in the wheel rattles most.
The wheel that's weak is apt to creak.
Is é an taobhlán is lofa is luaithe a níos gíoscarnach. [U]
The rottenest spoke(?) creaks the soonest.

"What a dust we kick up!" as the fly said to the cart-wheel.
"Nach mise a thóg an dusta?" arsa an cuileog i ndiaidh an chóiste. [U]
"Did not I raise the dust?" said the fly behind the coach.

An empty cart makes most noise.
Is é an carr folamh is mó a ní tormán. [U]

A car on the road earns money but two in the ditch earns nothing.

Short answers fit travelers.
["Fit" = befit, are suitable for.]

A rolling stone gathers no moss, but it gets a great shine.
Cha chruinníonn cloch chasaidh caonach. [U]
A turning stone gathers no moss.

The longest road has an end and the straightest road has an end.
Dá fhad é an bóthar, tagann a dheireadh. [C]
However long the road, its end comes.

The way to a friend's house is never long.

Pains and patience would take a snail to America.
Aimsir agus foighid, bhéarfadh sé an seilide go hIarúsailéim. [U]
Time and patience would take the snail to Jerusalem.

A merry heart goes all the way; a sad one tires er' a mile a'(way?).

Two shorten the road.
Giorraíonn beirt bóthar. [C]

It is a long lane that has no turn.
Is fada an bóthar nach bhfuil casadh ann. [U]
The road is long in which there is no turn.

It is a long road that has no public house!

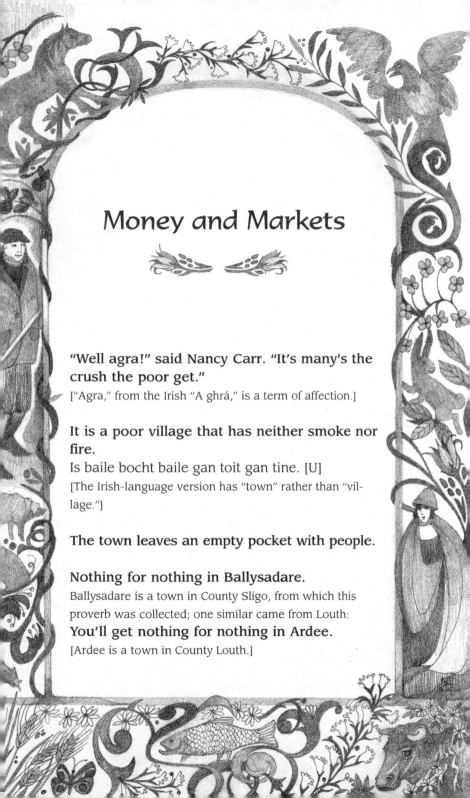

Money and Markets

"Well agra!" said Nancy Carr. "It's many's the crush the poor get."
["Agra," from the Irish "A ghrá," is a term of affection.]

It is a poor village that has neither smoke nor fire.
Is baile bocht baile gan toit gan tine. [U]
[The Irish-language version has "town" rather than "village."]

The town leaves an empty pocket with people.

Nothing for nothing in Ballysadare.
Ballysadare is a town in County Sligo, from which this proverb was collected; one similar came from Louth:
You'll get nothing for nothing in Ardee.
[Ardee is a town in County Louth.]

There's always money where there's dirt.

Money is like muck—no good till spread.

If you don't speculate you won't accumulate.

A wet day is a good one for changing a pound.
[On a wet day that is unsuitable for certain farmwork, the town could be visited to buy necessities.]

Money makes the horse gallop whether he has shoes or not.

Money would make the pot boil if you would throw ice in the fire.

A penny in a poor man's pocket is better than two pennies in a rich man's pocket.

One penny gets another.
Gheibh pingin pingin eile. [U]

You may not be talking of a penny when you have not a halfpenny.

Your pocket is your friend.
Is é do phóca do charaid. [U]

Your eye is your mark, your pocket is your friend; let the money be the last thing you'll part with.
["Your mark" = "your limit or guide"?]

Before you buy consult your purse.
Déan do mhargadh do réir do sparáin. [C]
Bargain according to your purse.

Don't buy a purse with the last half crown.
[A half crown was a silver coin, and there were eight of them to the pound.]

A wrinkled purse, a wrinkled face.

Never buy through your ears but through your eyes.

Taste and try before you buy.

You can never buy sweets for nothing.

What is not needed is dear at a farthing.
[A farthing was a small copper coin of little value. It took four to make up a penny.]

It is hard to pay for a loaf when you have it eaten.
Cha bhíonn cuimhne i bhfad ar arán ite. [U]
Bread that has been eaten is not remembered for long.

You can't have the hen and the price of her.
An té itheas an bhulóg, ní bhíonn sí fana ascaill aige. [C]
Whoever eats the loaf does not have it under his arm.

The thing that is bought dear is often sold cheap.
An rud a cheannaíthear go daor díoltar go saor é. [U]
The thing that is bought dear is sold cheap.

There are good goods in small parcels and poison in some.
Bíonn earraí maithe i mbeairtíní beaga. [C]
There are good goods in small parcels.

Good ware makes a quick market.

Don't bring all your eggs to the one market.
Ná cuir do chuid uibheacha uilig in aon bhosca amháin. [C]
Don't put all your eggs into one box.

Monaghan Day pays for all.
[Monaghan Day was held on February 25 in Mohill, County Leitrim. It was one of the biggest local fairs in County Leitrim, where the proverb was collected.]

If you have only a buck goat, be in the middle of the fair with him.
Mura mbeadh agat ach pocán gabhair bí í lár an aonaigh leis. [M]

No cow, no care, no errand to the fair.

There's no use in shouting in the fair when you have nothing to sell.

Ireland for a penny, but where is the penny?
Éirinn ar phingin; má tá, cá bhfuil an phingin? [U]
Ireland for a penny but, if so, where is the penny?

The Law

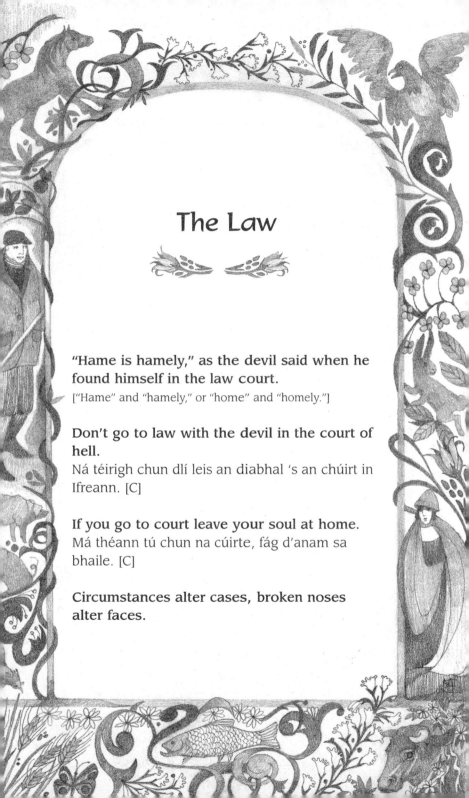

"Hame is hamely," as the devil said when he found himself in the law court.
["Hame" and "hamely," or "home" and "homely."]

Don't go to law with the devil in the court of hell.
Ná téirigh chun dlí leis an diabhal 's an chúirt in Ifreann. [C]

If you go to court leave your soul at home.
Má théann tú chun na cúirte, fág d'anam sa bhaile. [C]

Circumstances alter cases, broken noses alter faces.

A word in the court is worth a pound in the purse.
Is fearr focal sa chúirt ná punt sa sparán. [M]
A word in court is better than a pound in the purse.
A good friend in court is better than money in the purse.
Is fearr cara sa chúirt ná bonn sa sparán. [U]
A friend in court is better than a coin (called a "bonn") in the purse.

A pennyworth of law is enough for anyone.

Law is costly, shake hands and be friends.

Lawyers' houses are made of fools' heads.

A lawmaker is a law breaker.
Lucht déanamh dlí, chan cóir dóibh bheith a' briseadh dlí. [U]
Those who make laws should not break laws.

The law is no respector of persons.

Possession is eleven points of the law.
Ponc den dlí an tseilbh. [M]
Possession is a point of law.

New kings make new rules.

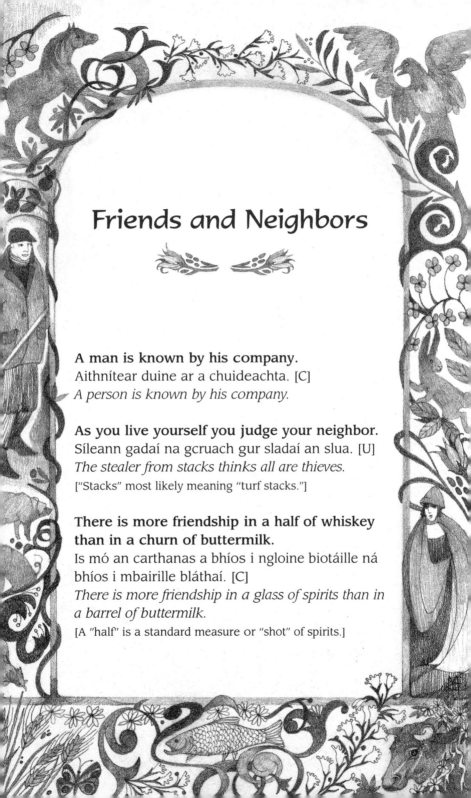

Friends and Neighbors

A man is known by his company.
Aithnítear duine ar a chuideachta. [C]
A person is known by his company.

As you live yourself you judge your neighbor.
Síleann gadaí na gcruach gur sladaí an slua. [U]
The stealer from stacks thinks all are thieves.
["Stacks" most likely meaning "turf stacks."]

There is more friendship in a half of whiskey than in a churn of buttermilk.
Is mó an carthanas a bhíos i ngloine biotáille ná bhíos i mbairille bláthaí. [C]
There is more friendship in a glass of spirits than in a barrel of buttermilk.
[A "half" is a standard measure or "shot" of spirits.]

Friends are like fiddle strings and they must not be screwed too tightly.

Don't be hard and don't be soft, and don't desert your friend for your own share.
Ná bí cruaidh agus ná bí bog; ná tréig do charaid ar do chuid. [C]

It is a pity on a man that is content in the troubles of his neighbors.
Is mairg a fhaigheann sólás i ndólás a chomharsan. [M]
Wretched is he who finds satisfaction in his neighbor's tribulation.

Now I have a cow and a horse, and everyone bids me good morrow.
An té a bhíonn suas óltar deoch air is an té a bhíonn síos luítear cos air. [M]
He who is up his health is drunk and he who is down is trodden upon.

Keep in with a bad person for a good person will never do you any harm.
Coinnigh an dhrochdhuine leat, is ní dhéanfaidh an duine maith dochar duit. [U]

Don't break your shins off your neighbor's pots.

Don't outstay your welcome like a neighbor's goat.
Cuairt ghearr is imeacht buíoch. [C]
A short visit and a thankful departure.

Come seldom, come welcome.
Ná téigh ach go hannamh go tigh do charad is gheobhair
fáilte. (Téigh ann go minic is beidh romhat deargchnáide.)
[M]
*Go only seldom to your friend's house and you will be wel-
comed. (Go often and you will be met with contempt.)*
Ní bhíonn fáilte roimh minic a thig. [C]
A frequent visitor is not welcomed.

Everyone is nice till the cow gets into the garden.
Bíonn gach duine lách go dtéann bó ina gharraí. [M]

Good mearings make good neighbors.
Fál maith a dhéanas comharsana maithe. [C]
[A mearing is a boundary between land owned by different people.]

If you want to know me come and live with me.
Níl eolas gan aontíos. [U]
There is no knowledge without cohabitation.

**Everybody is sweet to your face until you burn a stack of
turf with them.**
Tá chuile duine lách go gcaitear mála salainn leis. [C]
Everyone is pleasant until a bag of salt is used up with him.
[A stack of turf is a year's supply.]

Never want while your neighbor has it.

You can live without your own but not without your neighbor.
Tig leat déanamh gan do dhaoine féin; má tá, cha dtig leat déanamh gan comharsana. [U]
You can do without your own people but you cannot do without neighbors.

You have your neighbor when your friends are far away.
Más fada uait dho dhuine féin, is fearr dhuit do chomharsa. [C]
If your own people are far from you your neighbors are better for you.

In the previous and following proverbs the word "friend" is used in the sense of relation. The first is from County Cavan and the second from County Leitrim.

Your neighbor is your friend.
[The nearest to you when you need help.]

If you have not your neighbor you have nobody.

Don't take a slate off your own house to put on your neighbor's.
Ná bain tuí de do thoigh féin le sclátaí a chur ar thoigh fir eile. [U]
Don't take thatch off your own house to put slates on another man's.

If two neighbors want to fight they will find a quarrel in a straw.
Char fhadaigh dís tine gan troid. [U]
Two never lit a fire without a quarrel.

Strife is better than loneliness.
Is fearr imreas ná uaigneas. [C]

The war of friends doesn't last long.
Ní buan cogadh na gcarad. [C]

Never go between the skin and the tree.
Ná bí ag dul idir an craiceann is an crann. [U]
[Do not side with one relative against another.]

Kick him again, he's no relation!

Sports and Pastimes

One tale is good till another is told.
Is maith scéal go dtig scéal eile. [U]
A tale is good until another tale comes along.

One story brings on another.
Scéal a tharraingeas scéal. [C]

Never fly your kite too high.

Take the ball at the hop.
Beir ar an liathróid ar an gcéad phreib. [C]
Take the ball at the first hop.
["Hop" is another word for "bounce."]

The best swimmer is on the bank.
Is maith an snámhadóir a bhíos ar an mbóthar. [C]
The roadside swimmer is good.
He is a good hurler who sits on the ditch.
Is maith an t-iománaí an té a bhíonn ar an gclaí. [M]
The hurler on the bank is good.
The best footballer is always on the ditch.
Is maith an báireoir a bhíos ar an gclaí. [C]
The footballer on the bank is good.
The man on the grass is a good rider.
Is maith an marcach, an fear bhíos ar an talamh. [C]
The man on the ground is a good rider.
[A hurler is a player of the team sport called hurling, which is played
with a stick called a hurley and a small leather ball.]

It's hard to make a hunter out of an ass.
The world wouldn't make a racehorse of an ass.
Ní dhéanfadh an saol capall ráis d'asal. [M]

A cart horse could never win the Derby.

**The morning of the race is not the morning to feed your
horse.**
Tá sé rómhall croisín a chur faoi theach nuair a thiteas sé.
[U]
It is too late to put a prop under a house when it falls.

The racehorse throws his heels the highest.

The best horse doesn't always win the race.
Is minic nach é an capall is fearr a thóigeas an rása. [C]
Often the best horse doesn't win the race.

The lighter the jockey the swifter the horse goes.

"Diamonds for life!" said
the cardplayer's wife.

Spades for the bog.

One good trick is better
than twenty bad ones.
Is fearr cleas maith ná fiche droch-chleas. [C]

Cards and decks the devil's vice and jackstones worse
than all.
[Jackstones is a game of dexterity in which people gambled.]

The best throw of a dice is to throw it away.

Fair play is bonny play.
Fair play Chúige Uladh, triúr ar an bhfear! [C]
Ulster's fair play, three on one man!
[Interprovincial rivalry comes to the fore in this Connacht proverb!]

All play and no work leaves Jack a torn shirt.
[In proverbs, folktalkes, and other narratives, "Jack" is a common, or
stock, name.]

A shonin game is no game.
["Seoinín" implies "imported," "non-native."]

It is hard to get a good book for a bad reader.
A pun on the long established:
It is hard to get a good hook for a bad reaper.

Bad books are bad companions.

Dancing was first started by a madman.

Slips belong to dancing.

[A slip in a dance is a gliding step used, for instance, in the slip jig.]

Company brings the dogs to dance and night brings home the crows.

Préachán an tráthnóna. [M]

The evening crow.

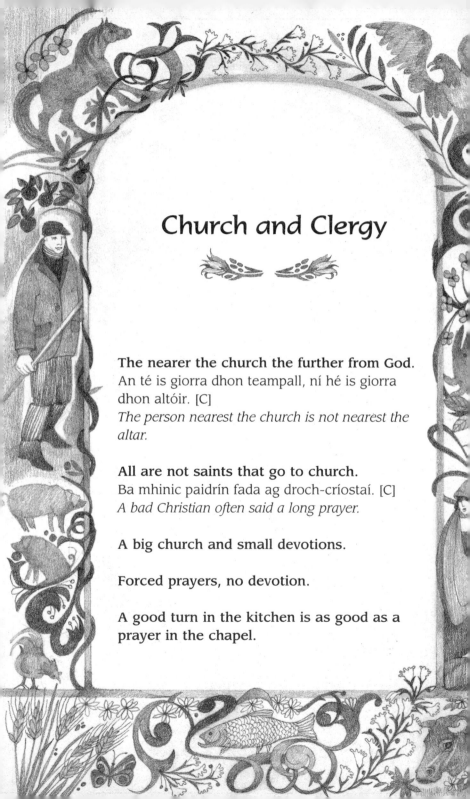

Church and Clergy

The nearer the church the further from God.
An té is giorra dhon teampall, ní hé is giorra
dhon altóir. [C]
*The person nearest the church is not nearest the
altar.*

All are not saints that go to church.
Ba mhinic paidrín fada ag droch-críostaí. [C]
A bad Christian often said a long prayer.

A big church and small devotions.

Forced prayers, no devotion.

**A good turn in the kitchen is as good as a
prayer in the chapel.**

Don't be too friendly with the clergy and don't fall out with them.
Ná bí róbheag is ná bí rómhór leis an gcléir. [M]
Neither be over-distant nor overfamiliar with the clergy.
Don't be in or out with the priests.
Ná bí mór ná beag le sagart. [C]
Be neither familiar nor distant with a priest.

Put the priest in the middle of the parish.
Cuir an sagart i lár an pharóiste. [M]
[This refers to the bygone custom of putting a basket of boiled potatoes
(the "priest") on a pot in the middle of the floor. The potatoes were then
eaten directly from it by those sitting around.]

A dumb priest never gets a parish.
Ní fhaigheann sagart balbh beatha. [M]
A dumb priest does not get a living.

It is a poor priest that has no curate.
Is bocht an sagart nach mbíonn cléireach aige. [U]

The habit does not make the monk.
Ní hé an t-éadach a ghníos an duine. [C]
Dress does not make the person.

**Patience and perseverance made a bishop
of his reverence.**
**Patience and perseverance won a wife
for his reverence.**
Faigheann bád foireann agus muirín ba.
[C]
A boat will get a crew and a family cows(?).

The minister christens his own child first.
Baisteann an sagart a pháiste féin a chéaduair. [U]
The priest baptizes his own child first.

A Sabbath well spent brings a week of content.

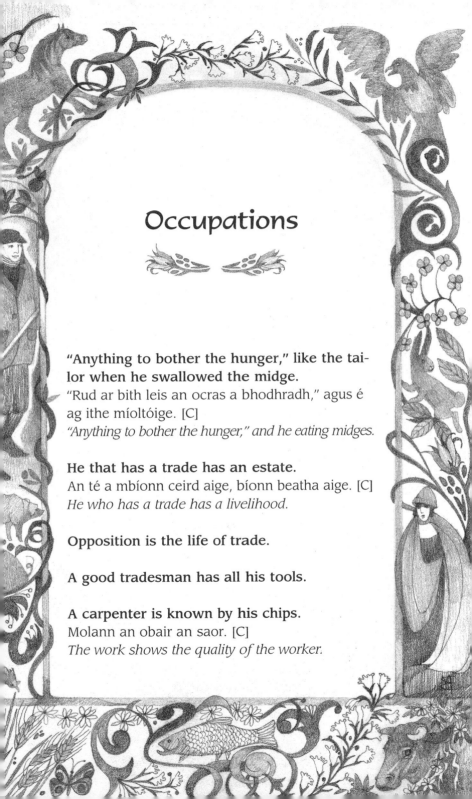

Occupations

"Anything to bother the hunger," like the tailor when he swallowed the midge.
"Rud ar bith leis an ocras a bhodhradh," agus é ag ithe míoltóige. [C]
"Anything to bother the hunger," and he eating midges.

He that has a trade has an estate.
An té a mbíonn ceird aige, bíonn beatha aige. [C]
He who has a trade has a livelihood.

Opposition is the life of trade.

A good tradesman has all his tools.

A carpenter is known by his chips.
Molann an obair an saor. [C]
The work shows the quality of the worker.

Though the carpenter is bad the splinter is good.
Más olc an saor is maith an scealbóg. [U]
Though the craftsperson is bad the splinter is good.

Old masons make good barrowmen.

A bad cobbler will never make a shoemaker.

If you knew everything you could be a doctor.

Charity covers a multitude of sins, but a tailor covers a multitude of sinners.

Never judge cloth by tailors' words.

Marry a tailor and you marry a thimble.

It would take nine tailors to hoist a bag of dust on a sow.
Ní bhíonn ins gach táilliúir ach an deichiú cuid d'fhear. [C]
Every tailor is only one-tenth of a man.

A tailor is known by his clippings.

A lazy tailor has always a long thread.
Snáithe fhada an táilliúir fhalsa.
[U]
The lazy tailor's long thread.

No odds among tinkers who carries the budget.

If "ifs" and "ands" were pots and pans there would be no need for tinsmiths' hands.

A tinker's wife and a tailor's wife are the two that never agree.
Bean táilliúra nó bean tincéara—sin beirt bhan ná réann le chéile. [M]

Everything goes in the beggar's bag.

It's a poor beggar that can't shun one door.
Is olc an bacach nach dtig leis toigh amháin a seachnadh. [U]
It's a poor beggar who can't shun a single house.

Carry a beggarman seven years, leave him down once and you never carried him at all.

When it is raining porridge the beggars have no spoons.

Beg from a beggar and you'll never be rich.
Bí ag iarratas ar dhuine bhocht, is ní bhfaighidh tú do shaibhreas a choíchin uaidh. [C]
Beg of a poor person and you'll never get your fortune from him.

Put a beggar on horseback and he'll ride to Cork.
Cuir bacach ar dhroim gearráin is rachaidh sé ar cos in airde. [U]
Put a beggar on horseback and he'll ride at a gallop.

The thief is no danger to a beggar.
Ní baol don mbacach an gadaí. [U]

Mór keeps herself and her maid looking for alms.

Cailín ag Mór is Mór ag iarraidh déirce. [C]

Mór with a maid and (even so) demanding alms.

[In proverbs, "Mór" is a a stock name for women as is "Morag" in Scottish Gaelic.]

Clothes and Appearance

"Nothing like a change of linen," as the old woman said when she turned her shift.
"Is deas an rud an ghlaine," mar a dúirt an bhean nuair a thiontaigh sí a léine i ndiaidh seacht mbliana. [U]
"Cleanliness is a fine thing," as the woman said when she turned her shift after seven years.

Beauty is only skin deep, ugliness goes to the bone.
Ní théann áilleacht thar an gcraiceann. [C]
Beauty does not go beyond the skin.

Beauty never boiled the pot and ugliness never thickened it.
Cha chuireann maise an pota ar gail. [U]
Beauty does not set the pot boiling.

What is beauty to comfort?

An inch is a great deal on a nose.
Is mór orlach de shrón duine. [U]
An inch is a great amount of a person's nose.

A crowl on a creepie looks nothing.
[Collected in County Cavan. A "crowl" here probably means an under-sized person or child, and a "creepie" is a wooden, usually three-legged, stool.]

A man is a man if he was rocked in a noggin.
[A "noggin" is a stave-built wooden vessel. Such wooden vessels of various sizes for various uses were once common, but perhaps the small ones used for drinking from are the ones in question here.]

Every fault is a fashion.

You might as well be out of the world as out of the fashion.
Bheadh sé chomh maith agat bheith as an tsaol is bheith as an fhaisiún. [U]

When a man's coat is threadbare it is easy to pick a hole in it.

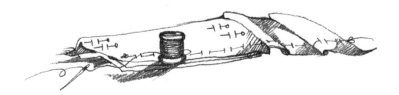

Many an honest heart beats under a ragged coat.
Is minic a bhí croí fíor fá chasóg stróicthe. [C]
There is often a true heart under a torn coat.

Charity covers a multitude of sins and an overcoat covers a multitude of rags.

Stitch by stitch the suit is made.
Tóigeann mion-chlocha caisleáin. [C]
Small stones build castles.

It's hard to tear a stocking across.

A coat twice turned is not worth sleeving.

A patch is better than a hole, but devil in it but that.
Is fearr paiste ná poll, ach níl ann ach san. [M]
A patch is better than a hole but only just.

Patch beside patch is neighborly but patch upon patch is beggarly.

Clothes make the man.
Is é an t-éadach a ní an duine. [U]

You cannot tell from a man's clothes how much he is making, but you must look at his wife's.

The shoemaker's wife and the blacksmith's horse often go unshod.
Is minic drochbhróga ar bhean gréasaí. [C]
The shoemaker's wife often has bad shoes.

He is no poor man that has two shirts.

It's a small smitch that spoils a Sunday shirt.
Is beag an rud a shalódh stocaí bána. [C]
It only takes a small thing to soil white socks.
[Collected in County Monaghan, where the meaning of "smitch" was given as "dirty spot."]

Many a white collar covers a dirty neck.
Síoda fighte ar mhuinín bhuidhe. [C]
Woven silk on a sallow neck(?).

The life of an old hat is to cock it, of an old shoe to black it.

When your hat is on, your house is thatched.
Nuair atá mo hata ar mo cheann, tá sclátaí ar mo thoigh. [U]
When my hat is on my head there are slates on my house.

Ill got, ill gone, like the old woman's bonnet.
An rud a gheibhthear go holc, téann sé go holc. [U]
What is got badly goes badly.

Fancy buys the ribbon but taste ties the bow.

You cannot take a glove off the hand that it is not on.
Is doiligh stocaí a bhaint d'fhear coslomnocht. [U]
It is difficult to take socks off a bare-footed man.

Pride without profit wearing gloves and going bare-footed.
A ring on the finger and not a stitch of clothes on the back.
Fál fán mhéar agus gan ribe fán tóin. [U]
A ring on the finger without a stitch on the backside.

Nan's dressed up and the wardrobe empty.
Síoda buí ar Shiobhán is na preabáin ar a hathair. [M]
Yellow silk on Siobhán and rags on her father.

Silks and satins, scarlet and velvet often put out the kitchen fire.

If you don't give me charity don't tear my coat.
Ach mur' dtabhara tú dada domh, ná stróc mo mhála. [U]
If you aren't giving me anything don't rip my bag.

It's no use giving an old pair of trousers if you pull the seat out of them.
When you give away your old breeches don't cut the buttons off.
Má thugann tú iasacht do chuid brístí, ná gearr na cnaipí díobh. [U]
If you lend your trousers do not cut the buttons off them.

You cannot take the britches off a Highlander.
Cad é a dúirt Goll ach gur deacair bríste a bhaint de thóin lom? [U]
What did Goll say but that it would be hard to take britches off a bare backside?
[Goll, whose chief attribute was strength, was one of Fionn Mac Cumhaill's Fianna or band of warriors.]

God's leather to God's weather.
[A comment collected with this proverb was that children should be allowed to go barefoot summer and winter—"God's leather" being skin.]

It is all the same to the man with the brogues where he puts his foot.
Is cuma le fear na mbróg cá gcuireann sé a chos. [M]

The beauty of an old shoe is to polish it.
Sean bhróg smeartha bróg nua. [M]
An old shoe polished is a new shoe.

Every man knows where the boot hurts him.
Is ag duine féin is fearr a fhios cén áit a luíonn a bhróg air.
[U]
A person himself best knows where the shoe presses on him.

Bad shoes are better than none.
Is fearr spré-mhóin ná bheith gan aon mhóin. [C]
Last year's peat is better than being without peat at all.

Never throw away the old boots till you get new ones.
Ná caith uait an tseanbhróg nó go bhfáighid tú an bhróg nua.
[C]
Do not throw away the old shoe till you get the new shoe.

Any fool carries an umbrella on a wet day but the wise man carries it every day.
Bhéarfaidh an fear críonna a chóta leis lá tirim. [U]
The wise man carries his coat on a dry day.

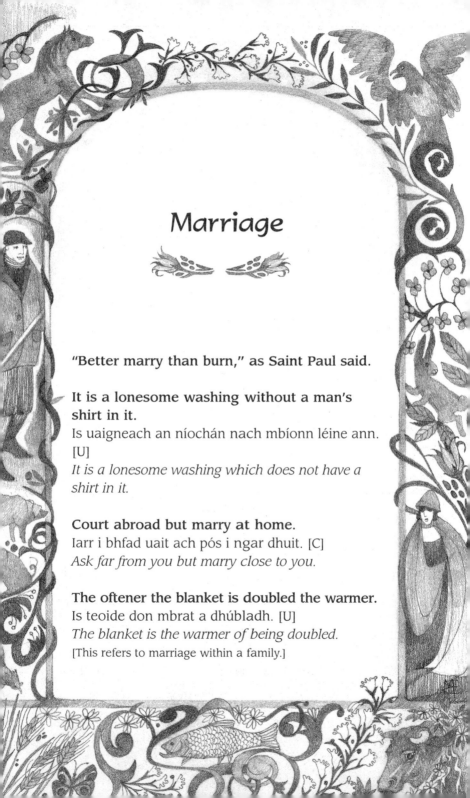

Marriage

"Better marry than burn," as Saint Paul said.

It is a lonesome washing without a man's shirt in it.
Is uaigneach an níochán nach mbíonn léine ann.
[U]
It is a lonesome washing which does not have a shirt in it.

Court abroad but marry at home.
Iarr i bhfad uait ach pós i ngar dhuit. [C]
Ask far from you but marry close to you.

The oftener the blanket is doubled the warmer.
Is teoide don mbrat a dhúbladh. [U]
The blanket is the warmer of being doubled.
[This refers to marriage within a family.]

Love the dunghill and you'll see no motes in it.
Má ghráíonn tú an t-aoileach ní fheicfidh tú drugann ann.
[U]

He who dotes in the dark sees no motes.
["To dote" is "to court."]

Three things you cannot comprehend:
the mind of a woman,
the working of the bees,
and the ebb and flow of the tide.
Na trí nithe is deacra a thuiscint:
intleacht na mban,
obair na mbeach,
tuile is trá na mara. [C]
The three hardest things to comprehend:
women's minds,
bees' work,
the flow and ebb of the sea.

There are matches for ciarogs.
Fághann ciaróg ciaróg eile amach. [C]
One beetle will locate another beetle.
[A "match" is a marriage partner and a "ciarog" is a kind of black beetle.]

Fits find each other.

There is never an old brog but there is a foot to fit it.
Níl aon tseanstoca ná faigheann seanbhróg. [M]
There is no old stocking that does not get an old shoe.
[A "brog," more often written "brogue," means a stout shoe and is from the Irish "bróg," for "shoe."]

Don't be too sure of your match like O'Foy.
Ná bí ró chinnte. [C]
Don't be too sure.

It is better to be refused for a hook on a harvest day than to be refused for a wife.

Marry a mountain woman and you will marry the mountain.
Pós bean tsléibhte is pósfaidh tú an sliabh uilig. [U]
Marry a woman from Truagh and you marry all Truagh.
[Truagh is County Monaghan's smallest barony.]
Pós bean ó Bhéara is pósfair Béara go léir. [M]
Marry a woman from Beara and you will marry all Beara.
[Beara is one of County Kerry's peninsulas.]

"That'll be the end of us all," as the old maid said when she saw the wedding.

Poor people must have poor weddings.

What is bound in harvest will be loosened in spring.
An phunann a cheangaltar sa bhfómhar scaoiltear san earrach í. [M]
The sheaf bound in harvest will be loosened in spring.
[Long ago the common time for weddings was in spring during the weeks prior to Lent. Marriage in autumn would not have been encouraged as there was little time to spare at the all-important harvest period. The metaphor is taken from binding the sheaves at harvest and loosening them later for threshing.]

There's no cure for love but marriage.
Níl leigheas ar an ngrá ach an pósadh. [C]

There is no feast till a roast and no torment till a marriage.

Ní céasta go pósta is ní féasta go róstadh. [M]

It's all better than a bad marriage.

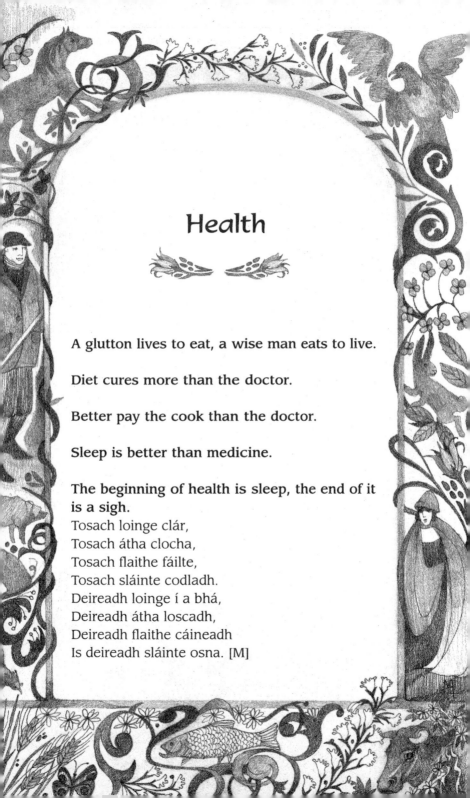

Health

A glutton lives to eat, a wise man eats to live.

Diet cures more than the doctor.

Better pay the cook than the doctor.

Sleep is better than medicine.

The beginning of health is sleep, the end of it is a sigh.
Tosach loinge clár,
Tosach átha clocha,
Tosach flaithe fáilte,
Tosach sláinte codladh.
Deireadh loinge í a bhá,
Deireadh átha loscadh,
Deireadh flaithe cáineadh
Is deireadh sláinte osna. [M]

The beginning of a ship is a plank,
The beginning of a ford is a stone,
The beginning of hospitality is a welcome,
The beginning of health is sleep.
The end of a ship is sinking,
The end of a ford is burning,
The end of hospitality is disparagement,
And the end of health is a sigh.

A dying rannie often lives longer than a sound man.
[In Irish, a "ránaí" means a "lank or thin person."]

A good laugh and a long sleep are the two best cures in the doctor's book.
Gáire maith is codladh fada—an dá leigheas is fearr i leabhar an dochtúra. [U]

A good laugh is as good as a day at the seaside.

A day in the country is worth a month in the town.

What butter or whiskey will not cure is incurable.
An rud nach leigheasann im ná uisce beatha, níl leigheas air. [U]

Whiskey when you're sick makes you well, whiskey makes you sick when you're well.

Doctors differ and patients die.

A light heart lives long.
Maireann croí éadrom i bhfad. [C]

A heavy heart seldom combs a gray head.
Cha chíorann tú ceann liath choíche. [U]
You will never comb a gray head.

Three places to be avoided:
a doctor's door,
a priest's door,
and a barrack door.
[A barrack door would be the door of a police barracks.]

Every cripple has his own way of walking.

Death

Never say die while there is meat on the shin of a wren.

A sick man reported dead always recovers.

You're late to run for the priest when the person is dead.
Chan é an t-am a dhul fán dochtúir nuair atá an duine marbh. [U]
It's not the time to go for the doctor when the person is dead.

Death and marriages make changes.
Éag is imirce a chloíos tíobhas. [U]
Death and flitting upset domestic economy.

Every day is a day nearer the grave.

Death takes the young as well as the old.
Níl fhios cé is luaithe, bás an tseanduine ná bás an duine óig.
[C]
There is no knowing which comes sooner, the old person's death or the young person's death.

Death never gives a year's warning to anyone.

Death comes like a thief in the night.
Tigeann an bás mar ghadaí san oíche. [C]

There is hope from the sea but no hope from the cemetery.
Bíonn súil le muir, ach cha bhíonn súil le cill. [U]

There is no cure or help against death.
Chan fhuil lia ná leigheas ar an bhás. [U]
There is no physician or cure for death.

Death is the poor man's doctor.
'Sé an bás leigheas an duine bhoicht. [C]
Death is the poor person's cure.

Death does not come without a reason.
Cha dtig an t-éag gan ceannfháth. [U]

What you think is worse than your death is perhaps for your good.
An rud is measa leat ná an bás, is leas dhuit go minic é. [U]
What seems worse than death to you is often for your good.

A wise man never saw a dead man.
Ní fhaca duine críonna duine marbh. [C]
A wise person never saw a dead person.

It is easy to pass by a dead man's door.
Is furaist gabháil thar dhoras duine mhairbh nuair ná bíonn
sé féin ná a mhadra istigh. [M]
*It is easy to go past a dead man's door when neither he himself
nor his dog is inside.*

It is easy to rob a dead man's house.
Is fuairste féasóg an leoin chuthaigh a stoitheadh nuair a
bhíonn sé féin marbh. [M]
It is easier to pull the fierce lion's beard when it is actually dead.

Sudden death, sudden mercy.

Luck

Luck's a king and luck's a beggar.

Luck and laziness go hand in hand.
Is minic a bhíos rath ar rapladh. [U]
There is often luck with laziness.

There is luck in leisure.

Good luck beats early rising.
Is fearr an t-ádh maith ná éirí go moch. [U]
Good luck is better than early rising.

Better to be fortunate than rich.
Is fearr sona ná saibhir. [U]

It's better to be lucky than wise.
Is fearr a bheith sona ná críonna. [U]

'Tis the fool has luck.
Bíonn áth ar amadán. [U]

Perseverance is the mother of good luck.

There is no luck where there is no correction.
Ní bhíonn an rath ach mar a mbíonn an smacht. [M]

Bad luck never comes its lone.
Ní tháinig trioblóid riamh ina haonar. [M]
Trouble never came on its own.
Dick died and the hen laid out.
"Ní thig an léan leis féin," mar dúirt an tseanbhean, nuair
cailleadh a fear 's rug an chearc amuigh. [C]
*"Woe does not come on its own," as the old woman said when
her husband died and the hen laid out.*

Good care takes the head off bad luck.
Baineann an coimhéad maith an ceann den tubaiste. [U]

The worse luck now the better again.

When luck comes it comes in a bucketful.
Nuair a bhíonns sé againn bíonn sé againn go tiubh, is nuair
a bhíonns muid folamh bímid folamh go dubh. [U]
*When we have it we have it in plenty and when we are bereft
we are totally bereft.*

The Supernatural

Speak to the devil and you'll hear the clatter of his hooves.
Trácht ar an diabhal agus taispeánfaidh sé é féin. [U]
Mention the devil and he'll appear.

It's time enough to shake hands with the devil when you meet him.
Ná beannaigh don diabhal go mbuaileann tú leis. [C]
Don't greet the devil until you meet with him.

Pulling the devil by the leg is a bad grip.
Ag tarraingt an diabhail de ghreim eireabaill. [C]
Pulling the devil by the tail.

It is easy preaching to the devil with a full stomach.

What comes in on the devil's back goes out on his horns.
An rud a fhaightear de dhroim an diabhail imíonn sé faoina
bholg. [M]

The devil will have his own.

It is a rocky road to heaven.

A good heart never went to hell.
Níor chuaigh fial riamh go hIfreann. [M]
Generosity never went to hell.

There's favor in hell and the biggest devil gets it.
Tá fábhar in Ifreann. [C]
There's favoritism in hell.

Banagher bangs the devil.
[Because of this and a similar expression, the place-name Banagher is
known far and wide. There are several Banaghers in Ireland, one being a
parish in County Londonderry and another a small town on the River
Shannon in County Offaly.]

It's hard to kill a bad thing.
Is doiligh drochrud a mharú. [C]

The devil couldn't kill a bad thing.

A chance shot may kill the devil.

When God comes in the door the devil flies out of the window.

God's help is nearer than the door.
Is foisce cabhair Dé ná an doras. [U]

God is good till morning.
Is maith Dia go lá. [U]
God is good till day.

The Lord never closed one door but He opened another.
Níor dhún Dia doras riamh nach bhfosclódh Sé ceann eile.
[C]
God never shut a gap but He opened another one.
Níor dhún Dia bearna riamh ná go n-osclódh sé ceann eile.
[M]
God never wets anything but He dries it again.

It is far away what God sends.
Is fada siar an rud a chuireas Dia aniar. [U]

God fits the back for the burden.
Chruthaigh Dia an droim i gcomhair an ualaigh. [C]

No ghost as bad as a live ghost.
Níl taibhse ar bith chomh holc le taibhse an dá chois. [U]
There is no ghost as bad as a ghost on two feet.

God is good and the devil is not bad either.

What the Pooka writes let him read it himself.
An rud a scríobhas an Púca, léadh sé féin é. [U]
[The Pooka is a solitary, malevolent supernatural creature that was believed to come out at night.]

FURTHER READING

For the classic account of proverbs, particularly European ones, their history, types and so on, see Archer Taylor in *The Proverb and "Index to the Proverb"* with an introduction and bibliography by Wolfgang Mieder, Bern, 1985.

For details of triads and other similar styles, see Fionnuala Williams in *Ulster Folklife*, Volume 34 (1988); Jonathan Bell, editor, "Triads and Other Enumerative Proverbs from South Ulster," pages 60–67.

For comparisons of some proverbs, see Fionnuala Williams in *Rosc, Review of Scottish Culture*, Number 6 (1990); Alexander Fenton, editor, "Irish versions of some proverbs found in Scots," pages 53–60.

For details of the way of life depicted in the proverbs, see the writings of E. Estyn Evans, such as *Irish Heritage: The Landscape, the People and their Work*, Dundalk, 1942, and the writings of Kevin Danaher, such as *In Ireland Long Ago*, Cork, 1962.

For American proverbs citing states and literary sources, see *A Dictionary of American Proverbs*; Wolfgang Mieder, editor-in-chief, Stewart A. Kingsbury and Kelsie B. Harder, editors; New York and Oxford, 1992.

For proverbs from seven continents, see Wolfgang Mieder, *The Prentice-Hall Encyclopaedia of World Proverbs*, New York, 1986.

INDEX

Key words are usually the first significant word, which is usually a noun but occasionally a verb or other part of speech. In the index, nouns are reduced to the nominative singular and verbs to the infinitive. For the words "man," "woman," "person," and "thing," which occur frequently, see under the accompanying adjective—for example, "hungry man" will be indexed under "hungry." In cases where there is no adjective, the noun or another more diagnostic word will be indexed. Similarly, in Irish, adjectives or other diagnostic words accompanying the common nouns—"fear" (man), "bean" (woman), "daoine" (person) and "rud" (thing)—will be indexed in preference. All personal and place-names, whether they are key words or not, are included in the index.

Key words in the English-language proverbs are in regular type.
Key words in the Irish-language proverbs are in italics.